Early L. & J. G. Stickley Furniture

FROM ONONDAGA SHOPS TO HANDCRAFT

L. & J. G. Stickley

EDITED BY DONALD A. DAVIDOFF, PH. D.,
AND ROBERT L. ZARROW

DOVER PUBLICATIONS, INC., *New York*

Copyright © 1992 by Dover Publications, Inc.
Preface copyright © 1992 by Robert L. Zarrow.
Introduction copyright © 1992 by Donald A. Davidoff.
All rights reserved under Pan American and International Copyright
Conventions.

Published in Canada by General Publishing Company, Ltd., 30 Lesmill
Road, Don Mills, Toronto, Ontario.
Published in the United Kingdom by Constable and Company, Ltd., 3
The Lanchesters, 162–164 Fulham Palace Road, London W6 9ER.

This Dover edition, first published in 1992, is a republication of all the
drawings and a selection of the photographs from a handbound salesman's catalogue, ca. 1906–9, and a set of retail plates, ca. 1909, produced
by the L. & J. G. Stickley Company, Fayetteville, N.Y. The preface by
Robert L. Zarrow and the introduction by Donald A. Davidoff were
written specially for this volume, and the price list was assembled from
handwritten notations in the catalogue.

Manufactured in the United States of America
Dover Publications, Inc., 31 East 2nd Street, Mineola, N.Y. 11501

Library of Congress Cataloging-in-Publication Data

Early L. & J. G. Stickley furniture : from Onondaga Shops to Handcraft /
    L.& J.G.Stickley: edited by Donald A. Davidoff and Robert L. Zarrow.
        p.   cm.
    ISBN 0-486-26926-4 (pbk.)
        1. L. and J. G. Stickley Inc.—Catalogs.   2. Furniture—United
    States—History—19th century—Catalogs.   3. Furniture—United
    States—History—20th century—Catalogs.   4. Arts and crafts
    movement—United States—Catalogs.   I. Davidoff, Donald A.
    II. Zarrow, Robert L.   III. L. and J. G. Stickley Inc.
NK2439.L2A4   1992
684.1′04′029474765—dc20   91-39894
                                                                   CIP

Contents

Preface

THE PLATES IN THIS VOLUME represent the furniture produced by the L. & J. G. Stickley Company from 1906 until 1909, from the end of their Onondaga Shops period through the beginning of their Handcraft period.

Three sources are reproduced here. The first is a catalogue depicting the final production of the Onondaga Shops. This catalogue, discovered recently in the basement of the Stickley factory, consists of hand-colored plates glued onto pages of black construction paper; it is the only copy in existence, as far as we know. Although the pieces illustrated include designs found in other catalogues, there is some new material. The catalogue shows three pieces with hand-carved floral-form panels: a stand, a desk and a chair (nos. 127, 408, 868). One example of the chair and one of the library table are known to exist; we are unaware of any examples of the stand, and since its image is on the reverse side of another picture it may have never been produced. (Other examples of hand-carved floral-form furniture, not pictured in this catalogue, include a settle belonging to Leopold Stickley [Fig. 5] and a hall seat found in the home of the company's treasurer, Charles M. Kessler.) Also of interest are the "cancelled" pieces, two china cabinets (nos. 653, 654). It is not known if these pieces were ever produced.

The second batch of source material is a set of photographs tipped in as an addendum to the catalogue. These photographs represent the first appearance of the L. & J. G. Stickley line of spindle furniture. Spindle furniture seems to have been much less favored by L. & J. G. than by Gustav Stickley; it appeared later (around 1909), was represented by only a few designs, and by 1912 had almost completely vanished from the catalogue. Consequently, it is much rarer than the Gustav Stickley spindle, and very few examples are known to exist. The most interesting of these spindle pieces are the Morris chair, no. 1273, and the footstool, no. 1292. Another interesting item is the settle, no. 1242, which appears to have been inspired by an early Gustav Stickley design (no. 172 from the 1902 retail plates); like the spindle furniture, this piece was made for only a short time.

The last of the source material is a set of loose retail plates apparently dating from 1909, which represents the first appearance of the Handcraft line. These plates include more examples of spindle furniture, the most interesting of which are the two even-armed settles, nos. 284 and 285. (Note that the numbering system for these later plates has changed from the four-digit scheme of the photographs to a two- and three-digit scheme, which was used for the remainder of the production.)

The continuum of designs contained in this volume, spanning the years from the last phase of the Onondaga Shops until the start of the Handcraft era, constitute the essential missing links in the early history of a corporation of substantial importance in the annals of American furniture.

Warren, New Jersey   ROBERT L. ZARROW

Introduction

A CRITICAL REEXAMINATION OF THE
WORK OF L. & J. G. STICKLEY

THE CONTRIBUTION OF THE FIRM OF L. & J. G. STICKLEY to the evolution and popularization of the design aesthetic of the American Arts and Crafts movement has long been underestimated. The oldest and best-known of the Stickley brothers, Gustav, was primarily responsible for the dissemination of the philosophy of John Ruskin and William Morris to a wide-ranging national audience (Fig. 1). Gustav left an enormous legacy, both in the actual furniture he produced and in his prodigious publications. Nonetheless, it remained for the superior business practices of his younger brothers Leopold (Fig. 2) and John George to place physical expressions of that philosophy in middle-class American homes and to revitalize the entire "mission aesthetic" for the second decade of the twentieth century. A critical reevaluation of their work has long been overdue.

Gustav Stickley played a seminal role in shaping the taste of a changing America. Furniture produced by his workshops not only represents classic American design,[1] but in some circles is considered to be the first original expression of American thought in furniture. Examination of Gustav's production over the sixteen years that his company existed independently reveals both his debt to the English cottage revival style and the subsequent stylistic modifications he made over that span of years. David Cathers, in his introduction to a Dover reprint of two catalogues[2] and his pioneering full-length study of the furniture of the American Arts and Crafts movement,[3] has provided a cogent sequen-

---

1. Thomas K. Maher, "Gustav Stickley's Early Furniture," *Arts and Crafts Quarterly*, vol. 2, no. 2 (Spring 1988): 7.
2. David M. Cathers, Introduction to Gustav Stickley and L. & J. G. Stickley, *Stickley Craftsman Furniture Catalogs* (New York: Dover, 1979).
3. David M. Cathers, *Furniture of the Arts and Crafts Movement, Stickley and Roycroft Mission Oak* (New York: New American Library, 1981).

Fig. 1. Gustav Stickley (1858–1942).

Fig. 2. Leopold Stickley (1869–1957).

vii

tial analysis of the design changes dividing Gustav's production into four distinct periods. A similar approach can be utilized to examine the work of Leopold and J. George.

Such an analysis of the furniture of L. & J. G. Stickley has only recently been attempted.[4] With few exceptions, its work has in recent years been maligned, regarded as derivative and not worthy of serious consideration. These misconceptions have derived from two sources. The first is the relative paucity of documentation of the firm's work. The second is the offhand dismissal in the ground-breaking Princeton catalogue of 1972.[5] In that influential catalogue of the show that sparked the current flame of interest in the Arts and Crafts movement, descriptions of some of L. & J. G. Stickley's furniture alluded to the use of inferior wood, the overuse of veneers and especially the derivative designs themselves. Thus, work by this company has been given relatively short shrift by the experts during the current revival. However, despite the critical writings that tended to disparage the furniture of L. & J. G. Stickley, the popular marketplace has always responded very favorably. The best of their settles, tall-case clocks and mantle clocks have consistently brought higher prices in recent years than similar examples from Gustav's workshops, underscoring the popular appeal of their work.

Gustav Stickley took great pleasure in delineating the changes in his furniture. He issued voluminous catalogues detailing both his design adaptations and the philosophical bases for those changes. His monthly magazine, *The Craftsman*, provided him with another outlet to further chronicle his views while simultaneously featuring his designs. In contrast, his brothers seemed less interested in selling a life-style and more focused on selling their furniture. Consequently they issued far fewer catalogues, none of which included anything like Gustav's essays on the Arts and Crafts aesthetic. Most of their catalogues were undated, with slip-in price lists so that each catalogue could be used for several years. Our knowledge of L. & J. G. Stickley's design philosophy derives only from hints provided by the brief introductions to the catalogues. Additionally, while many of Gustav's business records have been preserved, few of his brothers' records from the years 1900–1920 have been found. Thus, there has been much confusion over the work of L. & J. G. Stickley.

The present volume contains reprints of two catalogues from L. & J. G. Stickley's early transitional period that have recently come to light. This material not only fills a gap in the published information about that company's designs, but provides an essential underpinning to a more thorough understanding of its furniture in its relationship to the Arts and Crafts movement.

The importance of Leopold and J. George in the promotion of the Arts and Crafts aesthetic, especially in the second decade of the twentieth century, can be best understood once the history of the company has been briefly reviewed.

Though all the Stickley brothers worked together in various combinations during the last two decades of the nineteenth century, the relevant history for this reexamination begins with the founding of the United Crafts Workshops by Gustave (he later dropped the "e") Stickley in 1898. Leopold—familiarly known as Lee, just as Gustav was called Gus—was employed as shop foreman and principal representative of the company to the public.

George Clingman of Chicago's Tobey Furniture Company appreciated Gustav's production as it was unveiled at the Grand Rapids Furniture Show in July 1900. He quickly negotiated an exclusive arrangement whereby his firm would market Gustav's so-called New Furniture under the Tobey name.

4. Donald A. Davidoff, "The Work of L. & J. G. Stickley: The Mature Period and Design Sophistication," *Arts and Crafts Quarterly*, vol. 3, no. 1 (Winter 1989).
5. Robert Judson Clark, "L. & J. G. Stickley Co.," in R. J. Clark, ed., *The Arts and Crafts Movement in America 1876–1916* (Princeton, N.J.: Princeton University Press, 1972): 44.

It is likely that Gustav opted for anonymity in this venture because financial concerns were paramount for him at the moment. But with the favorable reviews his furniture had garnered in the trade journals, Gustav ended his arrangement with Tobey within six months. While the reason for this parting of the ways remains obscure, Gustav's later actions suggest that his independent nature made it difficult for him to tolerate the anonymous relationship with Tobey.

At this point, Leopold saw an opportunity and stepped into the vacuum left by Gustav's precipitous exit. He left United Crafts Workshops and purchased the former Collin, Sisson, and Pratt Factory in Fayetteville, New York, to start his own company. His first contract was to finish out the remainder of Gustav's contract with Tobey.[6]

Leopold adopted Gustav's original strategy of manufacturing furniture for other companies in order to place his own fledgling concern on a firm financial footing. Seemingly agreeable to relegating his name to anonymity, he contracted with many other companies. He continued to produce pieces for Tobey's next line of mission furniture ("New Furniture in Weathered Oak") that employed a broader design palette than had Gustav's original designs. By the summer of 1902 Tobey had added a less expensive line of mission furniture to its inventory and labeled it "Russmore";[7] Leopold produced pieces for this line as well. He also contracted with George Flint and Co., John Wanamaker, Jordan Marsh and Paine Furniture, among others.[8] Thus, while Leopold was not producing original designs, he nevertheless became a force to be reckoned with in the manufacture of mission furniture.

He soon recruited his brother J. George, who through his associations with Stickley and Brandt, the Binghamton firm that had formerly employed several of the Stickley brothers, had come to be known as "the best fancy rocker salesman in America."[9] By 1904 they had incorporated as the L. & J. G. Stickley Co., Inc., and begun production of their own furniture under the trademark "Onondaga Shops" (named after the county where the factory was located). Their first trade ad was placed in *Furniture World* in February 1904 (Fig. 3), and they exhibited for the first time at the gala 1905 Grand Rapids trade show. In March 1905, they issued their first catalogue.[10]

---

6. Donald A. Davidoff, "Sophisticated Design: The Mature Work of L. & J. G. Stickley," *Antiques and Fine Art*, vol. 7, no. 1 (December 1989): 87.
7. Sharon Darling, *Chicago Furniture, Art, Craft, and Industry 1833–1983* (New York: Norton, 1983): 235.
8. Davidoff, "Sophisticated Design," 87.
9. Cathers, *Furniture*, 70.
10. Ibid., 71.

Fig. 3. Advertisement from *Furniture World* (1904).

An examination of the production of the Onondaga Shops as shown in this volume will suggest some reasons why the work of L. & J. G. Stickley has been so underappreciated. Comparison with their brother Gustav's work shows that Leopold and J. George's work during this middle period was derivative and imitative. Often, when Leopold (from here on, "Leopold" should be understood to include J. George) did make design modifications, the results were crude or ungainly compared with Gustav's fine achievements. Occasionally, especially when the Onondaga Shops created pieces not in Gustav's repertoire, they triumphed. But regardless of design, the furniture of the Onondaga Shops is always extremely well made, utilizing the finest-grained quarter-sawn and fumed-finished white oak, and compares quite favorably in this respect with Gustav's early pieces.

In his creation of a new, original design aesthetic, Gustav shaped America's taste. He reveled in his role as the apostle of the new aesthetic. He sold not only furniture but a philosophy of living; his interpretation of the Arts and Crafts credo of surrounding oneself with "the art that is life" reverberated in everything he published and produced. Leopold eschewed the role of philosopher for that of the businessman. Perhaps for that reason, the Onondaga Shops furniture exhibits a less coherent aesthetic theme. Yet Leopold's early work cannot be dismissed simply because of its derivative nature. Whereas Gustav strictly adhered to the rule of rectilinearity, examination of the Onondaga Shops catalogue reveals less orthodoxy, as for example in chair legs that taper and others that terminate explosively in a Mackmurdo-style club foot. Oddly curved slats subdue rather than enhance the rectilinearity of some pieces. Also of interest are the crude attempts at plantlike low-relief decorative carving on some pieces, in contrast to the carefully integrated stylized inlays that Gustav utilized. This catalogue includes illustrations that suggest a line of carved furniture was planned. But almost all the hand-carved pieces rediscovered to date came from the basement of the factory itself or from the houses of the various officers of the company (Figs. 4, 5, 6), and it appears that, while Leopold occasionally made reference to carved pieces, he thought better of developing that line beyond some prototypes.

Fig. 4. Carved chairs from basement of L. & J. G. Stickley factory.

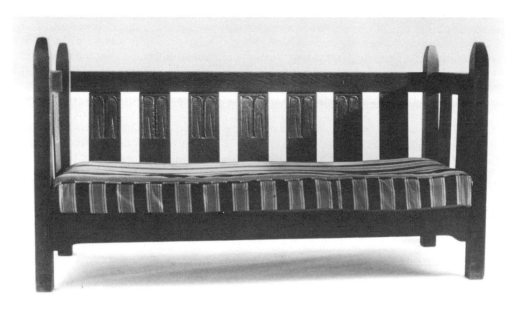

Fig. 5. Carved settle from Leopold Stickley's house. *Photograph courtesy of Butterfield & Butterfield, Los Angeles.*

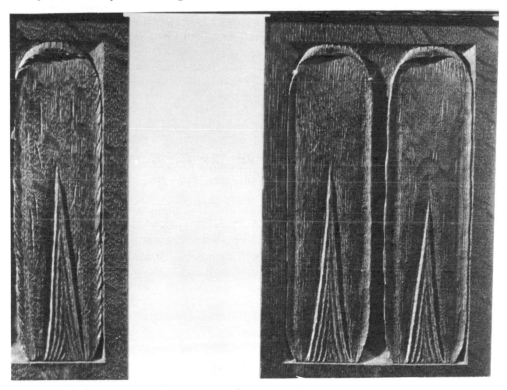

Fig. 6. Detail of carving on settle. *Photograph courtesy of Butterfield & Butterfield, Los Angeles.*

Whereas Gustav's designs, at least during his early and middle periods, were always true to his philosophy of design, ornamentation and handwork, Leopold apparently felt free to adopt or reject bits and pieces of his brother's design principles whenever he felt it economically useful to do so. Thus, when Gustav was successfully marketing the virtues of handwork, Leopold labeled his 1905 catalogue "Handmade Furniture." But his next catalogue downplayed this notion and instead simply focused on the "frank construction" of the furniture. Leopold experienced no contradiction in stating in the same paragraph that "some of this furniture has quaint cuttings in place; some has metal work to accent certain points, and some has an outline so simple and devoid of ornament as to be almost severe in its plainness."[11] He tried to cover all bases and provide middle-class America with whatever *it* wanted. Unlike Gustav, he made no attempt to create a movement or mold America's aesthetic sense.

In late 1906, Leopold changed the name and shopmark of his furniture from "Onondaga Shops" to "Handcraft." After this change was announced in the Oct. 25th issue of *Furniture World*, no further advertisements appeared for a year. Until the catalogue and retail plates reproduced here were discovered, it was assumed that the L. & J. G. Stickley Company issued no further catalogues until 1910.

The catalogue and retail plates reproduced here graphically illustrate the varied directions Leopold had considered taking (including the aforementioned line of carved furniture) as well as the new influences that ultimately shaped his production for the second decade of the century. The linkages between the two furniture lines are seen in the photographs of the prototypes of his new Handcraft furniture (see pp. 105–12), photographs tipped in at the end of the Onondaga Shops catalogue and numbered with the Onondaga Shops production numbers. With the publication of the Handcraft retail plates, these prototypical pieces, in new drawings, were renumbered according to a new schema.

The development of these prototypical pieces marked a new maturity for the work of L. & J. G. Stickley and a pivotal turn in the commercial Arts and Crafts aesthetic. The new designs exemplified a fresh approach whose roots could be stylistically traced to three sources—the Prairie style of Frank Lloyd Wright, the European Reform Movement espoused by the Viennese architect-designers and the English Arts and Crafts masters such as Voysey, Mackmurdo and Gimson. The synthesis of these disparate influences revitalized the simple mission style and pushed the firm of L. & J. G. Stickley into a new prominence in the marketplace. Though the full realization of this new aesthetic would only reach fruition over the next several years, the work reproduced in the Handcraft retail plates does illustrate the roots of these designs.

Furthermore, quality workmanship was reemphasized. Quarter-sawn white oak was the rule, and older factory workers have handed down stories that Leopold would personally inspect each shipment of lumber when it arrived and reject those boards which did not meet his standards. The factory also developed a laminating technique to enhance the remarkable tiger-striped grain pattern of the quarter-sawn oak on all four sides of furniture legs, rather than on just two sides as with nonlaminated legs. All pieces were fumed to further highlight the grain pattern, and even those critical of L. & J. G. Stickley's designs have always acknowledged the superb quality of the finish.

It is probable that much of the innovation seen in the Handcraft designs can be traced to Leopold's engaging of the 29-year-old Peter Heinrich Hansen as chief designer in 1909 (Fig. 7). Hansen was a German-born cabinetmaker who emigrated to the United States at the turn of the century and went to work for Gustav Stickley around 1904. There he met

---

11. "Some Sketches of Furniture Made at the Onondaga Shops" in Stephen Gray, ed., *The Mission Furniture of L. & J. G. Stickley* (New York: Turn of the Century Editions, 1989): 44.

Fig. 7. Peter Hansen (1880–1947).

and married his fellow worker Ruth Ann Williams, a Chicago-trained draftsperson originally from upstate New York. Following a monetary dispute with Gustav, the couple moved to Fayetteville, where Peter was hired by Leopold to be both shop foreman and chief designer. Leopold's second wife, Louise, confirmed that Peter was instrumental in designing L. & J. G. Stickley's furniture.[12] And work definitively attributed to Peter Hansen (e.g., a mantle clock and three entire houses) tangibly demonstrates that he was conversant with all of the major thematic influences evidenced in L. & J. G. Stickley's mature work.

The photographs and Handcraft catalogue drawings reproduced in this volume help provide the historical bridge from the derivative middle period of the Onondaga Shops to the sophisticated Handcraft designs of the mature period. Among the more important pieces produced during these transitional years are the first of a line that reflects the Prairie-style aesthetic of Frank Lloyd Wright. The early examples of this line, which would culminate in the quintessential paneled and spindled Prairie settles of 1912–13,[13] include the spindled Morris chair (no. 473), settles (nos. 284, 285) and tall-back chairs (nos. 304, 312, 320, 382, 384) reproduced here.

Curiously, a connection between Frank Lloyd Wright and Leopold Stickley had long been a subject of speculation. It was formerly rumored that Leopold's company, in its earliest years, produced the furniture for Wright's Bradley and Hickox houses. David Hanks ultimately put that rumor to rest by establishing that the firm of John Ayres had actually made the furniture.[14] Some of the confusion probably originated from the fact that Wright allowed his clients to put Leopold's furniture in secondary rooms of some of his commissioned houses. There was certainly a similarity between Wright's ideals of geometric simplicity and the proper role of the machine in the production of high-quality

12. Cathers, *Furniture*, 84.
13. Stickley, *Stickley Catalogs*, L. & J. G. Stickley catalog, 24, 27.
14. David A. Hanks, *The Decorative Designs of Frank Lloyd Wright* (New York: Dutton, 1979): 41.

furniture and Leopold's own philosophy as expressed in his 1914 catalogue.[15] The compatibility of some of L. & J. G. Stickley's furniture with the Prairie style was noted by other architects of the Prairie School; both Purcell and Elmslie and Walter Burley Griffin followed Wright's example in allowing Leopold's furniture a place in houses they designed (Fig. 8).

Examination of the L. & J. G. Stickley Prairie-style pieces reveals that some are direct adaptations of Wright designs, such as the Prairie settle and chair inspired by the settle in the 1909 Robie House (Figs. 9, 10). Other pieces are less derivative and instead merely reflective of the principles underlying Prairie School design. The work illustrated here represents the transition to those design principles. While none so focus on "carefully calculated horizontality" to evoke the "long horizon line of the prairie [itself]"[16] as would the soon-to-be-produced Prairie settle, many of the pieces illustrated here do rely on the square spindle, found so ubiquitously in the work of the Prairie School architects. As Don Kalec has pointed out, these spindles served "as a definite link between the furniture and architecture" in that they supported "a sense of visual privacy without bottling up the ever free flowing space."[17]

---

15. Stickley, *Stickley Catalogs*, introduction to L. & J. G. Stickley catalog.
16. Donald Kalec, "The Prairie School Furniture," *Prairie School Review*, vol. 1, no. 4 (Fourth Quarter, 1964): 6.
17. Ibid., 12.

Fig. 8. Living room in house by Walter Burley Griffin, with furniture by L. & J. G. Stickley.

Fig. 9. Prairie settle. *Photograph used by permission of Christie's, New York.*

Fig. 10. Prairie chair. *Private collection.*

The Morris chair, no. 473 (Fig. 11), exemplifies these aesthetics. It is similar to Wright's 1903 Willits House armchair (Fig. 12) in that the transparency created by the spindles blurs the vertical boundaries without impeding the eye. The L. & J. G. Stickley chair, however, adheres perhaps even more strictly to Prairie-style principles by working only in horizontals and verticals, avoiding the curves seen in Wright's piece. The transparency of the Stickley piece is further enhanced by grouping the spindles in the center and leaving open space on either side. Furthermore, this piece was designed as a Morris chair, with an adjustable back for individual comfort.

The latter notion of comfort is one element that distinguishes the furniture produced by L. & J. G. Stickley from that designed by many of the Prairie School architects. Since the company was in business to sell furniture, comfort was the primary design consideration. In his introduction to the 1914 catalogue, Leopold emphasizes that "chairs are studied

Fig. 11. Morris chair (no. 473) by L. & J. G. Stickley.

Fig. 12. Willits House chair designed by Frank Lloyd Wright. *Photograph used by permission of Christie's, New York.*

from the point of view of many different sitters" and "care is given to your comfort."[18] In contrast, Wright designed furniture primarily to complement the designs of his houses. And, according to Brendan Gill, "Wright himself confessed that his shins were often rendered black and blue through unlucky encounters with chairs of his design."[19] Some of the other Prairie School architects were less ideological than Wright and at least attempted to design chairs that served the function of sitting. But it might be said that one contribution of the L. & J. G. Stickley firm was the "simple" synthesis of comfort with design.

Architects of the Prairie School emphasized simple geometric form and natural materials, and designed furniture that focused on the simple circle, square, hexagon and octagon. The Handcraft retail plates reproduced here likewise present many examples of furniture designed with this pure geometric focus (see, e.g., the table, no. 564, and the tabourette, no. 560). And when Wright attempted to create a visual privacy screen with his tall-backed dining chairs, L. & J. G. Stickley, following his lead, manufactured a variety of similar chairs.

18. Stickley, *Stickley Catalogs*, introduction to L. & J. G. Stickley catalogue.
19. Brendan Gill, *Many Masks: A Life of Frank Lloyd Wright* (New York: Putnam, 1987): 494.

The Handcraft retail plates also show pieces that have roots in the Viennese Secessionist movement (see, e.g., the book stand, no. 48) and in the work of the English architect-designers (see the smoker's table, no. 515). The development of extensive furniture lines incorporating these influences would, like the integration of the Prairie style, be fully realized by the time the 1914 catalogue was issued. The cross-fertilization of these styles through Peter Hansen's skill resulted in such masterworks as his mantle clock—a subtle blend of Voysey-like design with Prairie School traits that produced a unique Arts and Crafts ideal (Fig. 13).

Fig. 13. Mantle clock designed by Peter Hansen. *Photograph used by permission of Skinner's, Boston.*

These fresh designs with their synthesis of broad influences, together with Leopold's consummate business skill, pushed the firm to ever-increasing financial success. Gustav, in contrast, financially overextended himself and filed for bankruptcy in March 1915; by May 1916 he was essentially out of business. The Stickley family, led by Leopold, formed Stickley Associated Cabinetmakers in 1917 in an apparent attempt to stave off Gustav's financial ruin. The new firm included Leopold as president and Gustav as vice president, with other brothers as the other officers. Gustav's independent nature, however, soon manifested itself again; he worked for the new concern only for twelve months, then retired to the family house in Syracuse and never returned to the furniture market.

Leopold proved to be more adaptable. Because he only produced and sold furniture, not a philosophical package, he was able to sense the changes occurring in America's furniture tastes. An unpublished catalogue reveals that as early as 1916 he had begun the manufacture of oak reproductions of Shaker furniture. While price lists show that he was still selling mission furniture in 1925, he had begun a phaseout by 1918. His first catalogue of Cherry Valley furniture, showing colonial revival pieces, was issued in 1924, by which time actual production of mission pieces had ceased.

The L. & J. G. Stickley Company continues in business today, and until 1985 it occupied the same Fayetteville factory that Leopold had bought in 1901. In 1989, the company began to reissue many adaptations of the unique mission pieces from both the L. & J. G. Stickley and the Gustav Stickley catalogues.

If the L. & J. G. Stickley Company had only made relatively inexpensive versions of Prairie-style furniture, no matter how comfortable, or if it had merely refined some of Gustav's designs, its contribution to the Arts and Crafts movement could be ignored. But these catalogues clearly show that, in addition to being financially successful, the company was able to produce a variety of furniture exemplifying original and sophisticated design. Through the fortunate hiring of Peter Hansen, the firm of L. & J. G. Stickley infused the Arts and Crafts movement with a synthesis of compatible styles, tangibly disseminating the aesthetics of the Prairie School, the geometry of the Viennese Secessionists and the elegance of the English designers to the American middle class. The furniture of Leopold and J. George Stickley ultimately achieved a subtlety beyond that of their older brother Gustav, and much of their work can be regarded equally as classics of American design.

The author gratefully acknowledges the help of Susan Tarlow, Paul Fiore, Ray Stubblebine, Cathie Zusie, Olive (Bets) Hansen, John King, Bob Zarrow, Marcia Ehlers, Mike Danial, Bruce Johnson and Jeanne Rice.

Cambridge, Massachusetts   DONALD A. DAVIDOFF

Salesman's Catalogue, ca. 1906–9

Price List

On the first two sets of material, from the unpublished salesman's catalogue, prices have been penciled in on many of the plates. Many individual pieces have two prices (for a given size) and a few have three. These apparently apply to the different wood options: mahogany, oak and maple. All the prices shown on the plates are listed below.

NUMBER	DESCRIPTION	MAHOGANY	OAK	MAPLE
Drawings				
314	bench		$ 4.50	
331	bookcase	$30.	24.	
350	table	22.50	12.50	
375	table	18.	13.	
377½	table		18.30	
379	table	27.	15.	
380	round table	9.	8.50	
381	round table	11.	9.50	
384	round table (48″)	27.	15.	
384	round table (54″)	30.	17.	
396	round table	25.	15.	
397	table	15.50	9.50	
400	desk	26.	24.	$ 18.
400½	desk	34.	24.	
402	desk	16.50	12.	
404	desk	19.50	18.	14.
405	desk	34.	24.	
406	desk	11.25	10.50	8.
507	tea table		4.75	
508	tea table		4.75	
516	book table	18.	16.50	13.
516	book table	15.50	14.	10.50
518	table	15.25	13.75	9.75
601	gong		11.	
618	table (48″)		18.50	
618	table (54″)		21.50	
618	table (60″)		24.50	
625	chair	5.	4.50	
626	chair	7.25	6.50	
629	china cabinet		35.	
632	sideboard		62.	
637	sideboard		47.	
640	server		18.	
642	china cabinet		37.	

646	china cabinet		31.
712½	Morris chair	21.	18.
738	settle	27.50	25.
742	daybed	38.	32.50
745	settle	27.50	25.
751	rocker	11.	9.
751½	rocker	15.50	13.50
754	chair	7.50	6.50
760	chair	19.50	16.50
761	rocker	19.50	16.50
764A	chair		6.
770	Morris chair	19.	16.
775	settle	60.	55.
778	chair	8.25	7.50
778½	chair	12.25	11.
779	rocker	8.25	7.50
779½	rocker	12.25	7.50
780	chair	12.50	11.
780½	chair	17.	15.
781	rocker	12.50	11.
781½	rocker	17.	15.
810	settle		20.
858	chair	10.	8.50
859	rocker	10.	8.50
887	rocker	11.75	10.25
888	chair	11.75	10.25
890	chair	15.50	12.50
922	daybed	33.	28.
1150	chair	11.50	
1151	rocker	11.50	
1152	table	21.	16.

Photographs

1202	chair	8.	6.50
1203	rocker	8.	6.50
1204	chair	7.	5.
1205	rocker	7.	5.
1239	settle (48″)	21.	16.50
1239	settle (60″)	46.	42.
1242	settle (60″)	46.	42.
1242	settle (72″)	52.	47.
1321	rocker	11.50	7.50
1326	chair	11.50	7.50

4

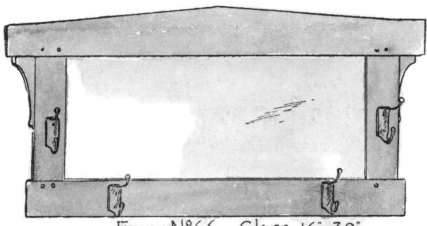

Frame Nº 66   Glass 16"x 30"

Nº 127
47 High, 14 Top
Oak and Mahogany. Hand Carved

Nº 128
44" High 14"x14"

6

Nº 131
12" × 12"
7" High

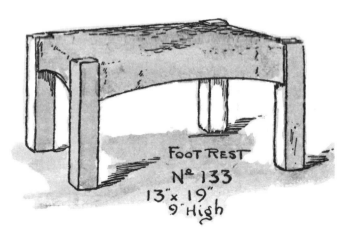

FOOT REST
Nº 133
13" × 19"
9" High

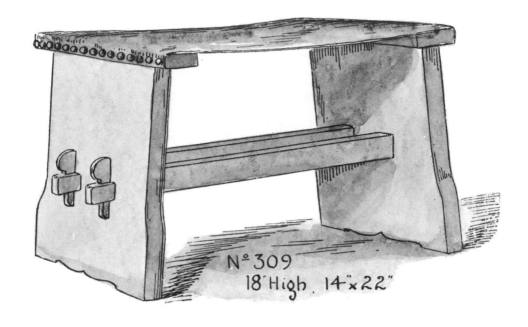

Nº 309
18"High. 14"x22"

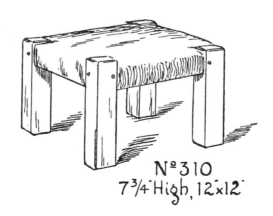

Nº 310
7¾"High, 12"x12"

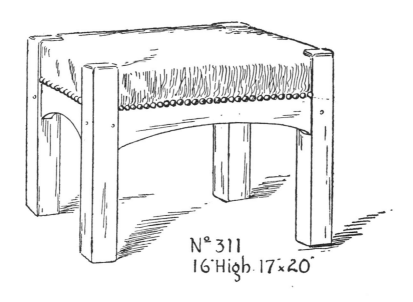

N.º 311
16" High. 17"x20"

N.º 314
19" High, 14"x22"

Nº 324
13" Top, 28 High

Nº 325
13" Top 22" High

10

Nº 326 Open. Nº 326½ Closed.
56" High, 30" Wide, 12" Deep

N.º 327 Open. N.º 327 ½ Closed
56" High, 36" Wide, 12" Deep

Nº 328 Open. Nº 328½ Closed.
56" High, 49" Wide, 12" Deep

No 331 OPEN   56"HIGH , 70"WIDE 12"DEEP

14

Nº 342
30"×48"
Leather only

Nº 346
42"High, 21"Wide

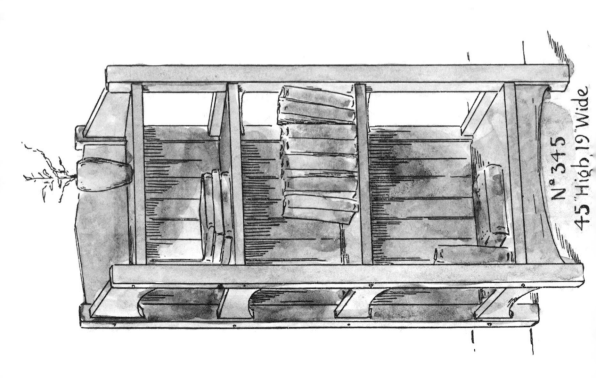

Nº 345
45"High, 19"Wide

16

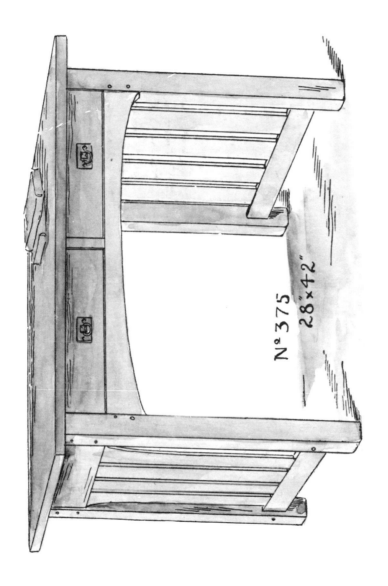

Nº 375
28"×42"

Nº 376. 30"×42"

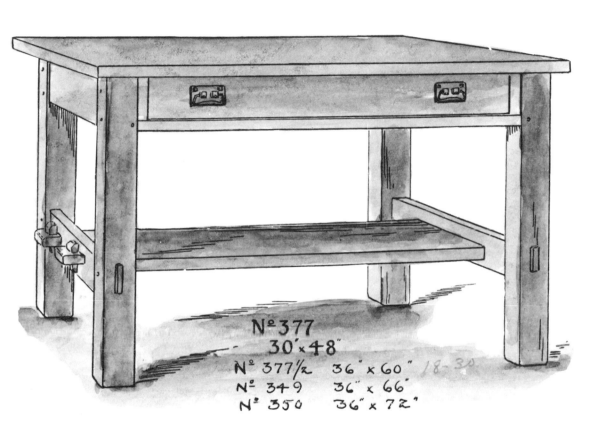

Nº 377
30"x 48"
Nº 377½   36" x 60"   18-30
Nº 349   36" x 66"
Nº 350   36" x 72"

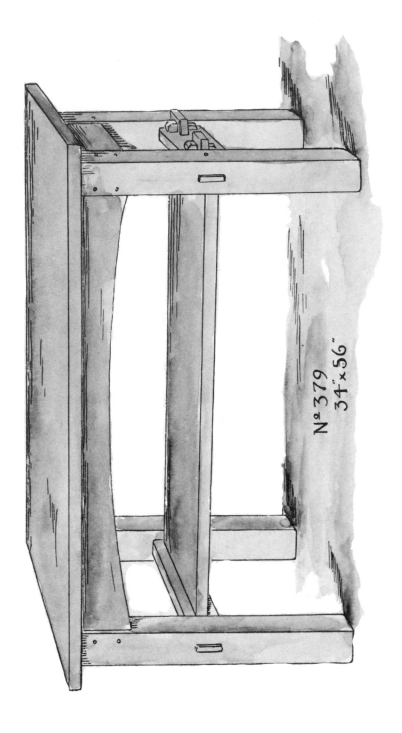

N⁰ 379
34"×56"

Nº 381. 36"

Nº 380. 30"

21

N° 383
48"

Nº 384
48" and 54"

Nº 387
16"x16"

Nº 388
36"

24

Nº 394
4.5"×72"

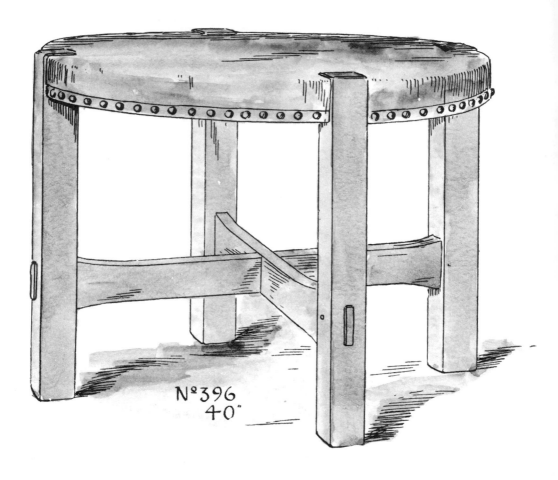

Nº396
40"

Nº397

.28"×40"

Nº 399

30"x48"

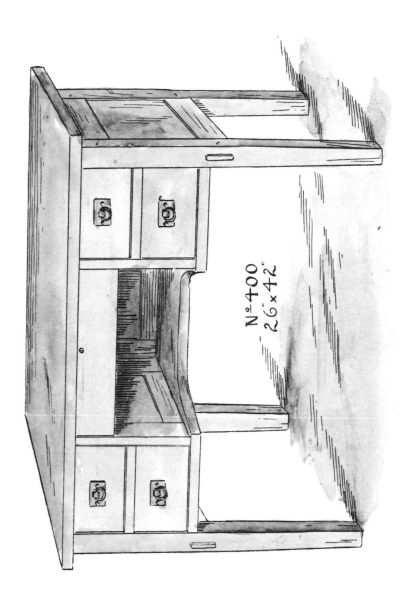

Nº 400
26"x42"

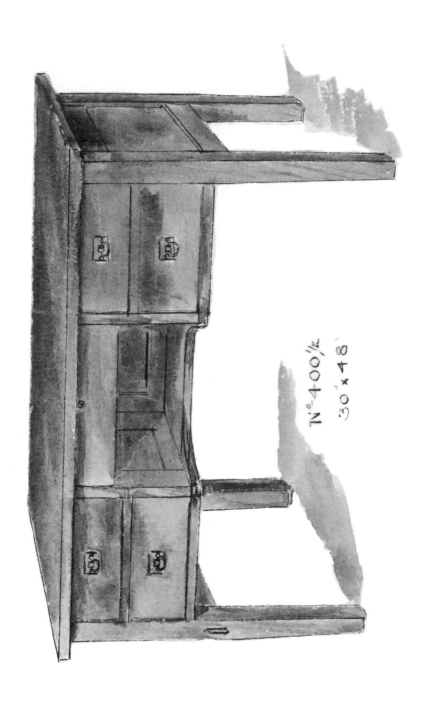

N°400½
30'×48'

30

Nº 401
20"x 34"

Nº 402
22"×40"

N.º 404
22"x40"

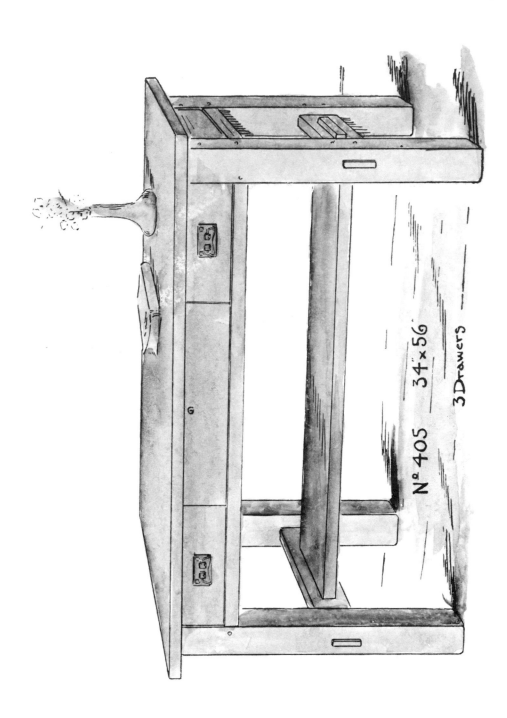

Nº 405   34"×56"

3 Drawers

34

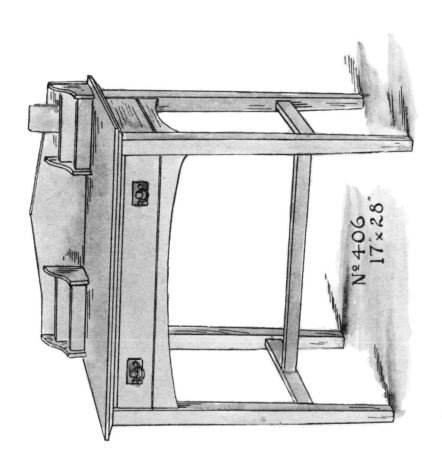

Nº 406
17"×28"

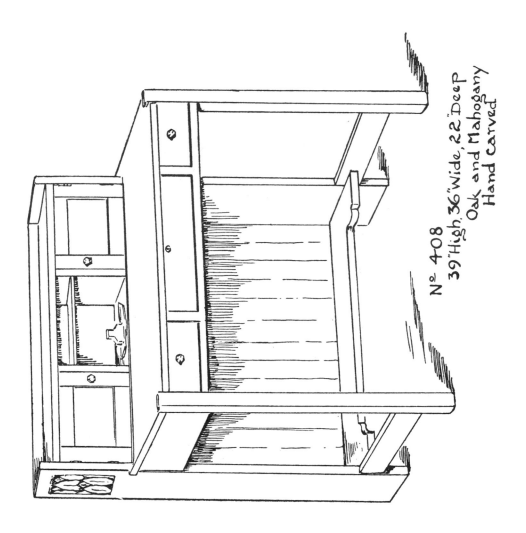

Nº 408
39"High, 36"Wide, 22"Deep
Oak and Mahogany
Hand Carved

Nº 411
32"x60"

Nº508
24"High, 24"Top

Nº507
24"High   17"x26"

38

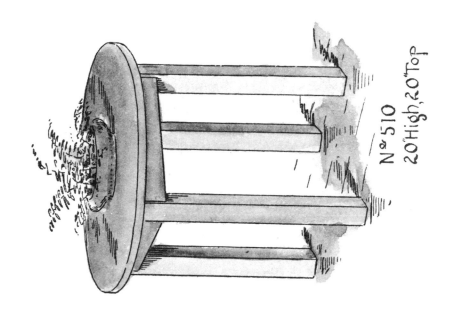

N⁰ 510
20"High, 20"Top

N⁰ 509
20"High 16"×16"

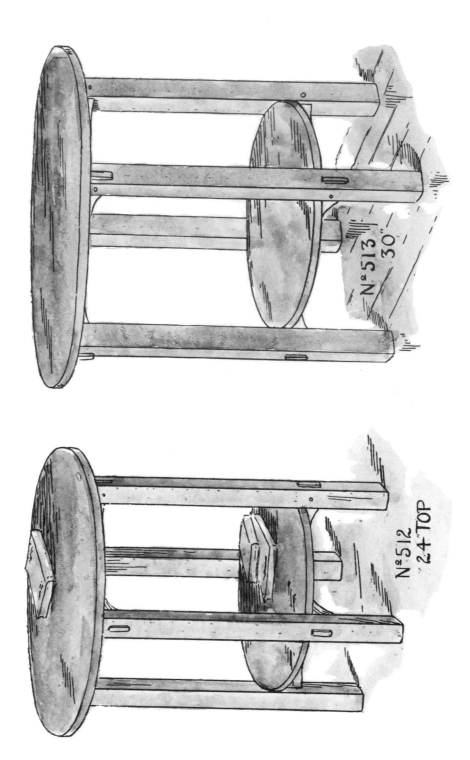

Nº 513
30"

Nº 512
24" TOP

Nº 516

27″ × 27″
Oak and Mahogany

41

Nº 518
24" x 40"
Oak and Mahogany.

42

Nº601
34" High
21" Wide
15" Deep

43

N° 618

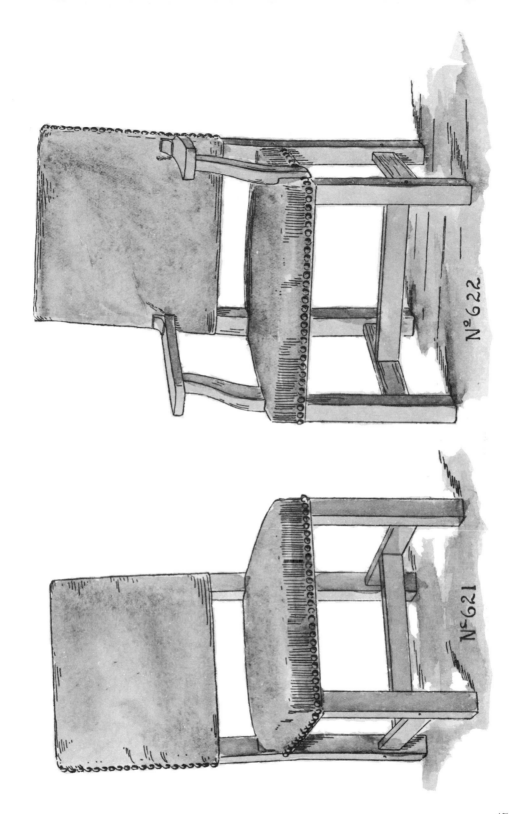

Nº 622

Nº 621

45

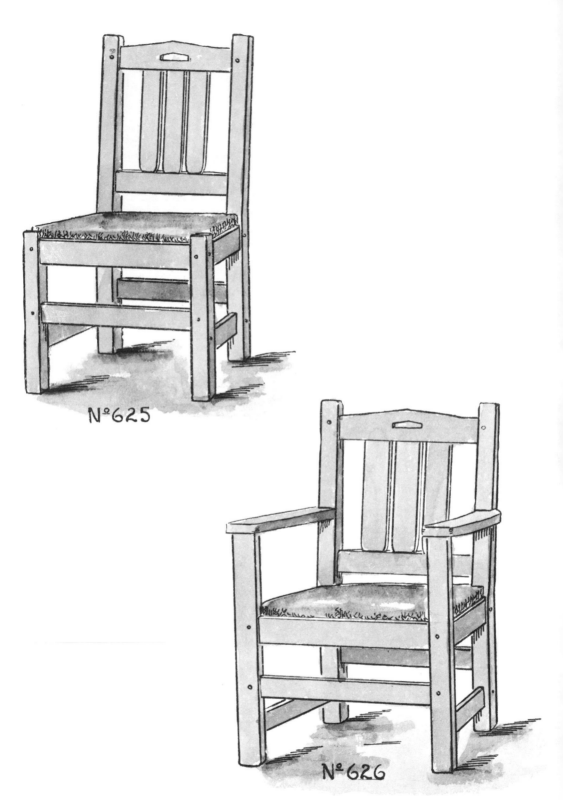

Nº 625

Nº 626

Nº 629
70"High. 47"Wide. 16"Deep

Nº 632
62" High, 72" Long, 25" Deep
Glass 12" x 51"

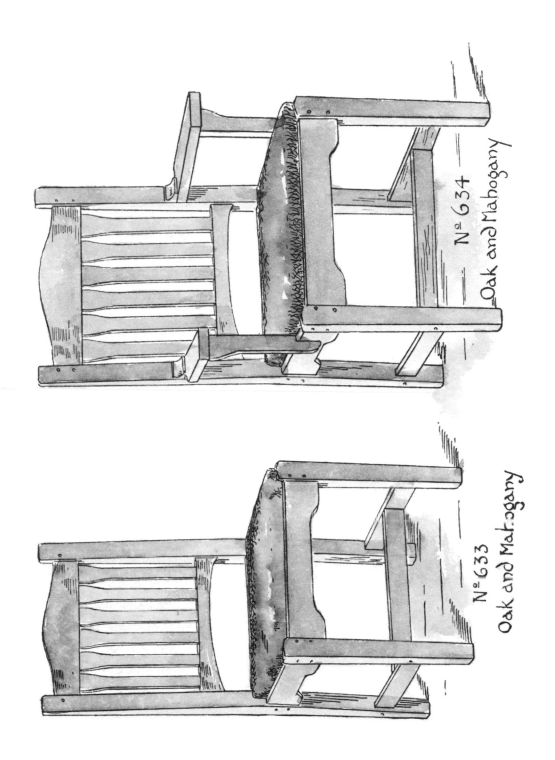

Nº 634
Oak and Mahogany

Nº 633
Oak and Mahogany

49

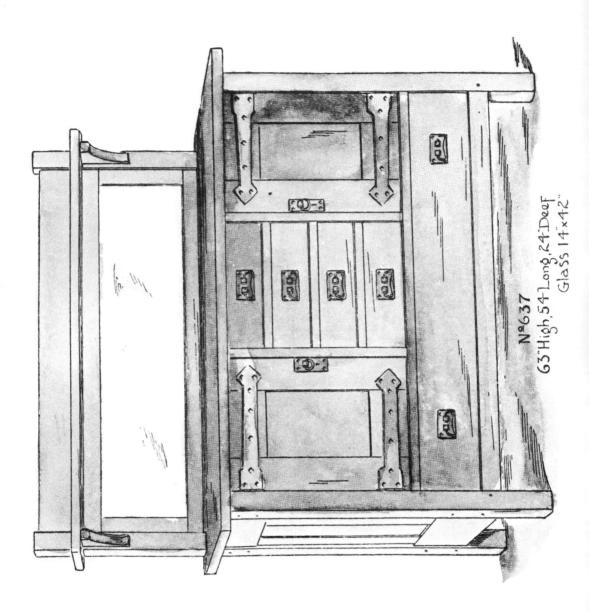

Nº637
63"High, 54"Long, 24"Deep
Glass 14"x42"

Nº 640
4'9"High 4'8'Long 2'2"Deep

Nº641
44˝High.44˝Long.18˝Deep

Nº 642
69"High, 51"Wide, 17"Deep

Nº 646
70" High, 44" Wide 16" Deep

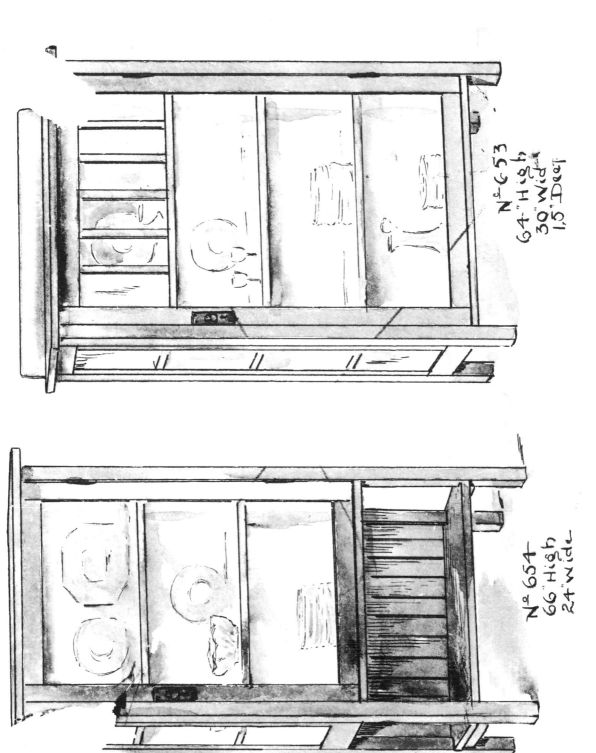

No 653
64" High
30" Wide
1.5" Deep

No 654
66" High
24" Wide

№ 712/2

56

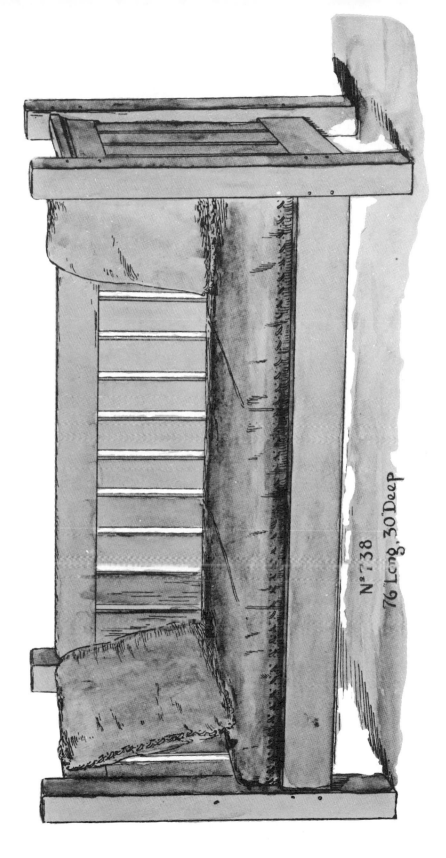

Nº 738
76" Long, 30" Deep

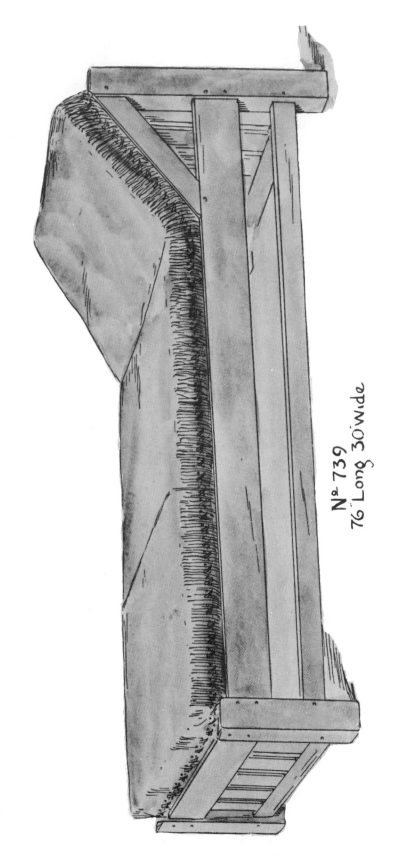

Nᵒ 739
76" Long 30" Wide

58

Nº741
40" Long, 24 Deep

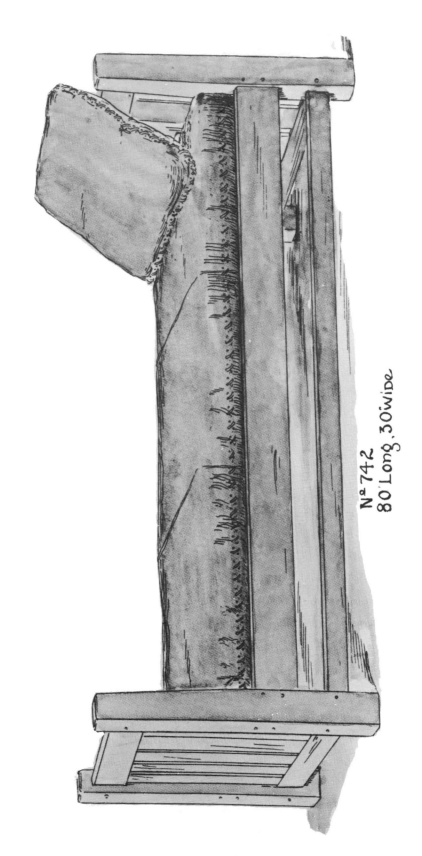

Nº 742
80' Long, 30" wide

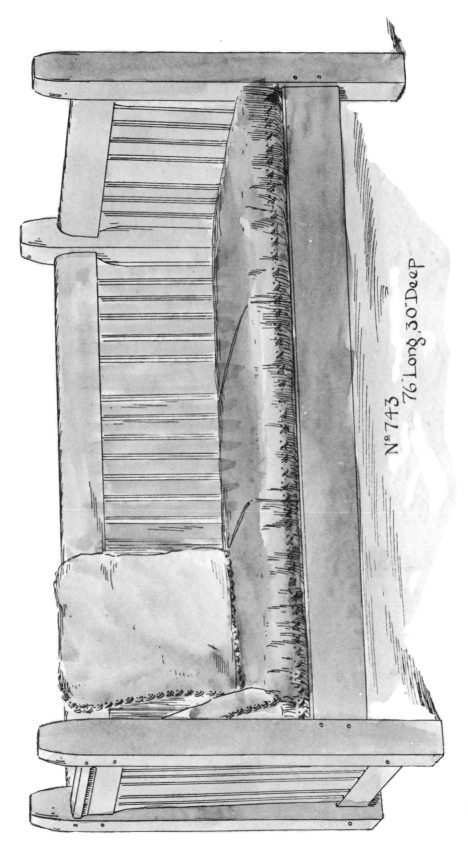

Nº 743

76' Long, 30" Deep

61

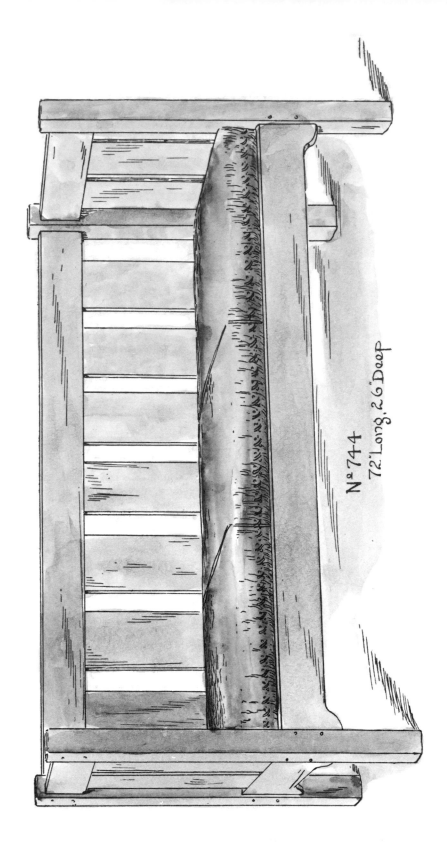

Nº 744
72" Long, 2'6" Deep

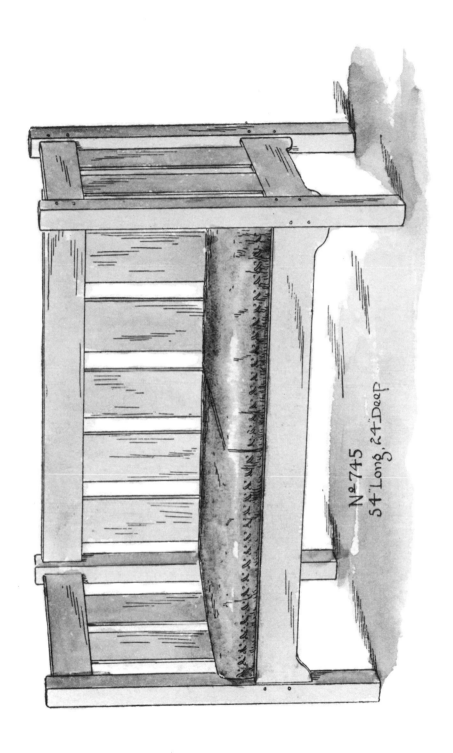

Nº 745
54" Long, 24" Deep

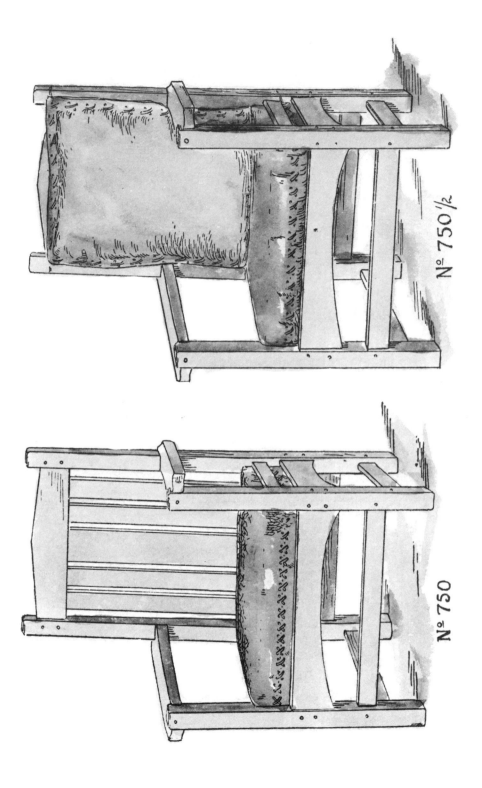

Nº 750 ½

Nº 750

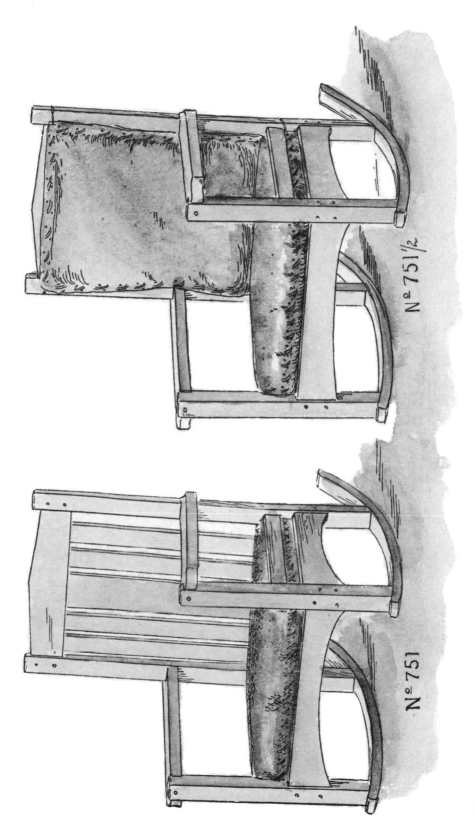

Nº 751½

Nº 751

65

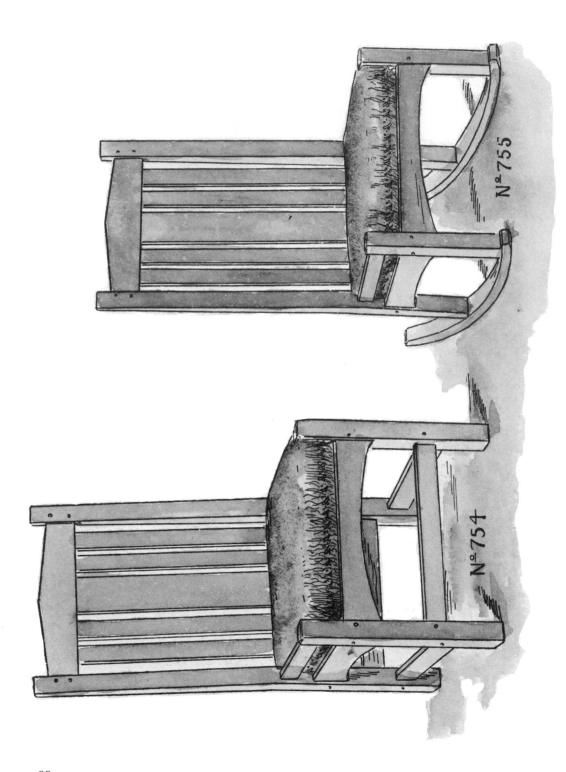

Nº 755

Nº 754

N.º 760

N° 761

Nº 762

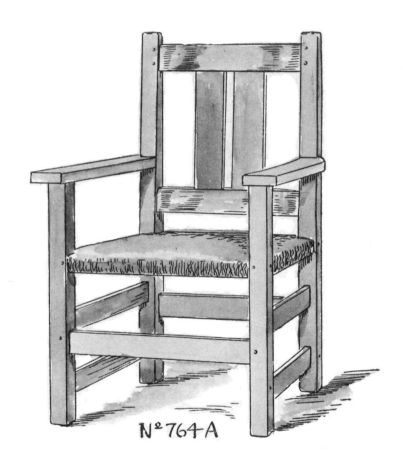

Nº 764A

Nº 762

Nº 769

Nº 770

Nº 772

N° 774

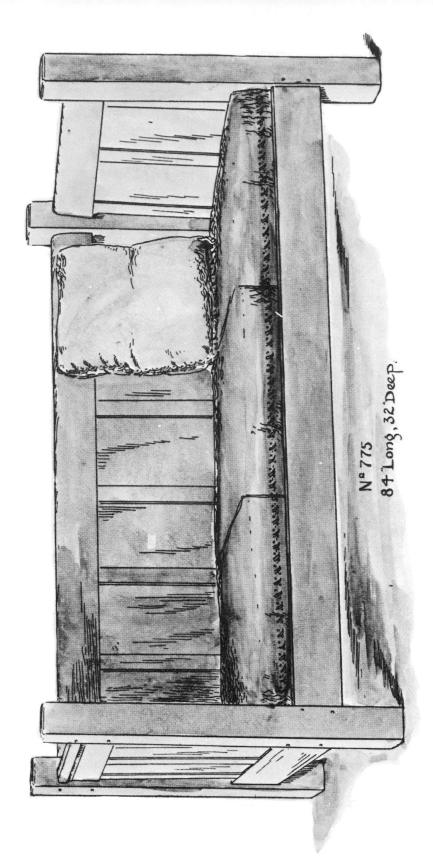

Nº 775
84" Long, 32" Deep.

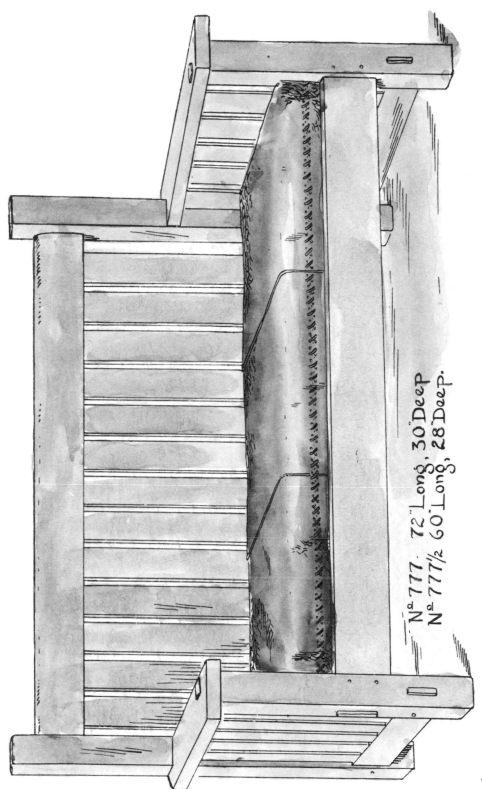

Nº 777. 72"Long, 30"Deep
Nº 777½ 60"Long, 28"Deep.

77

N° 778½

N° 778

78

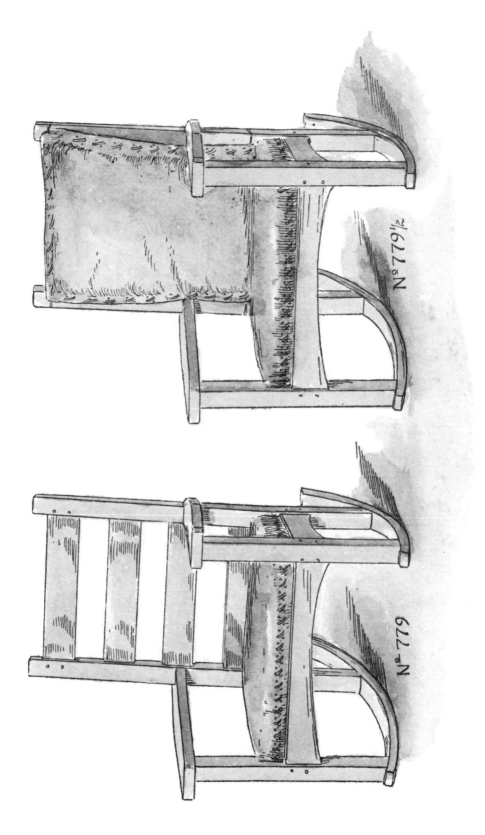

No 779½

No 779

79

Nº 780

Nº 780½

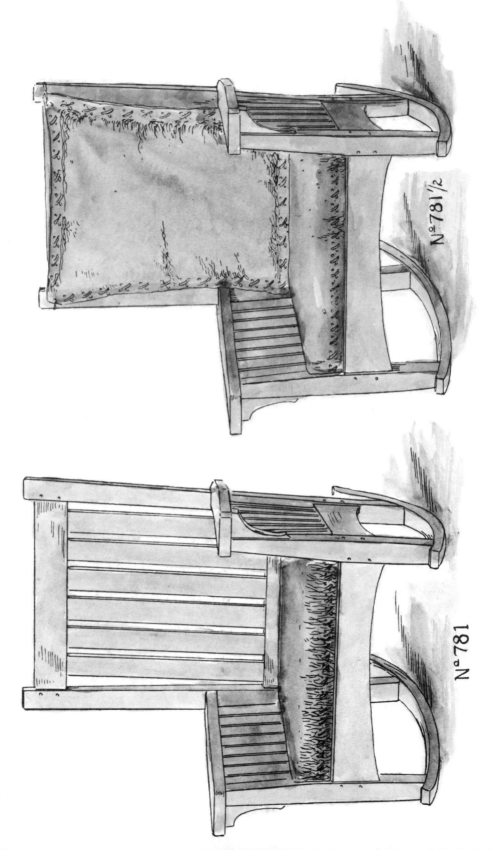

No 781½

No 781

82

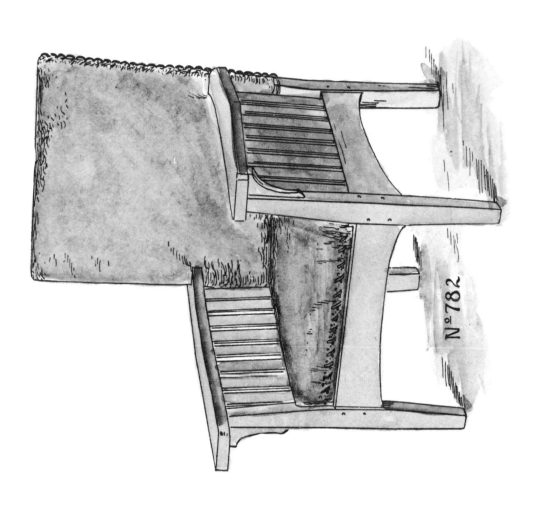

N.º 782

83

N° 783

Nº 785
44"Long, 22"Deep

Nº 788

Nº 790
Adjustable Back

Nº 798

Nº 809
37 High, 42"Long, 18"Deep

Nº 810

37″ High, 54″ Long, 20″ Deep

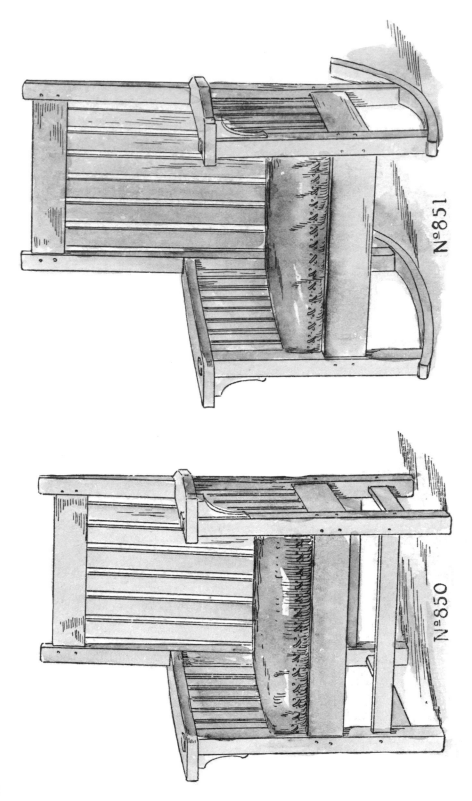

№851

№850

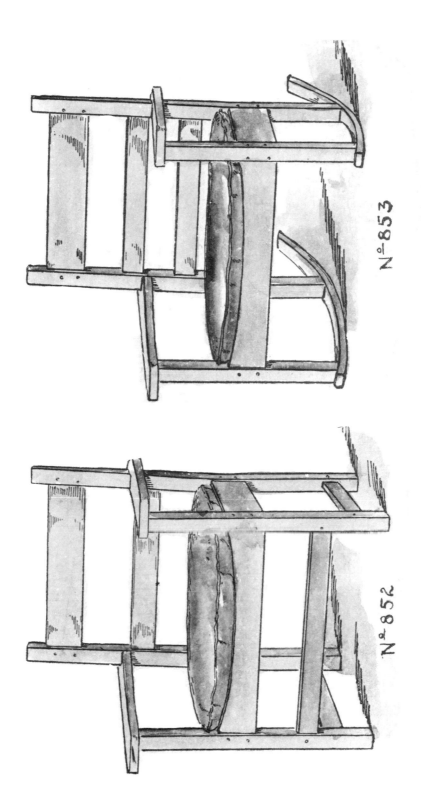

N° 853

N° 852

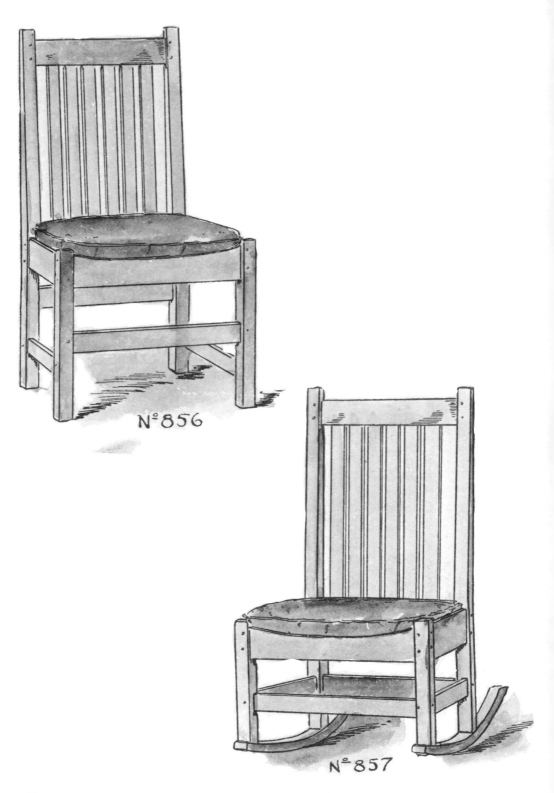

Nº 856

Nº 857

N° 858

N° 859

Nº 868

Oak and Mahogany

Hand Carved

Nº 872

Nº 873

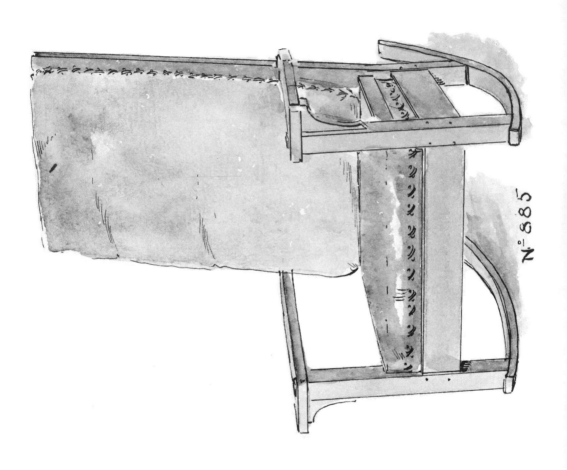

N.º 885

98

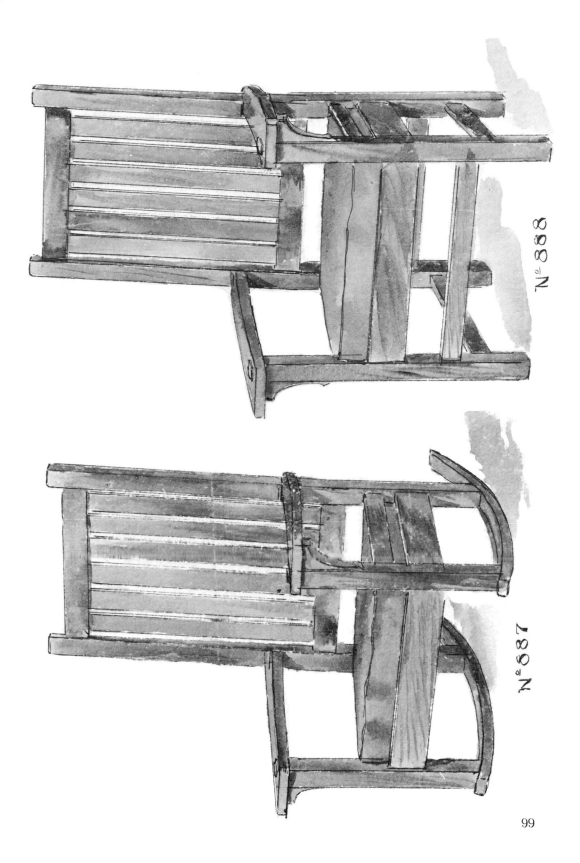

Nº 888

Nº 687

99

N° 890

N° 922
28'H. 72'L. 27'W

101

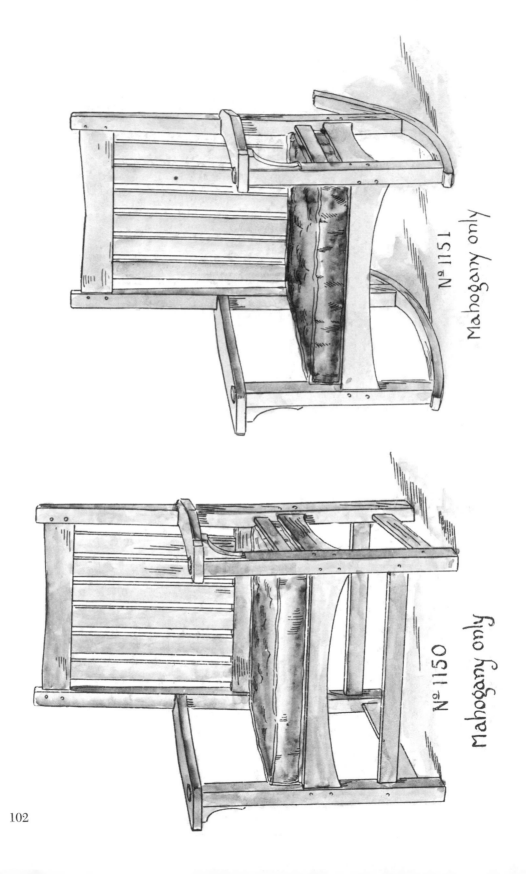

Nº 1151
Mahogany only

Nº 1150
Mahogany only

102

Nº 1152. 30"×48"
Oak and Mahogany

Nº 1155
Mahogany only

Nº 1154
Mahogany only

1203

Height of back 37"
  "   " Seat 15"
  Size "   15"x15"

1202

Height of back 42"
  "   " Seat 18"
  Size " 15"x15"

1205

Height of back 37"
" " Seat 16"
Size " " 15" x 15"

1204

Height of back 42"
" " Seat 18"
Size " " 15" x 15"

106

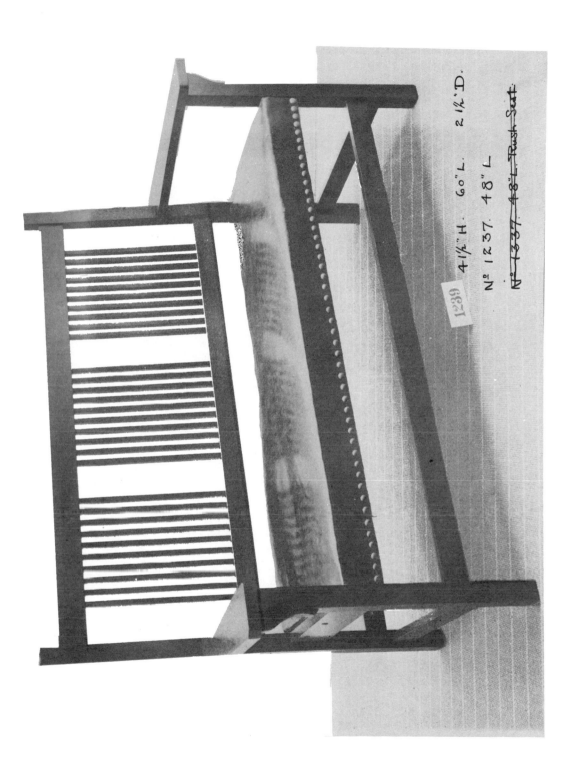

41½"H. 60"L. 2½"D.

Nº 1237. 48"L

Nº 1237. 48"L. Rush Seat.

1239

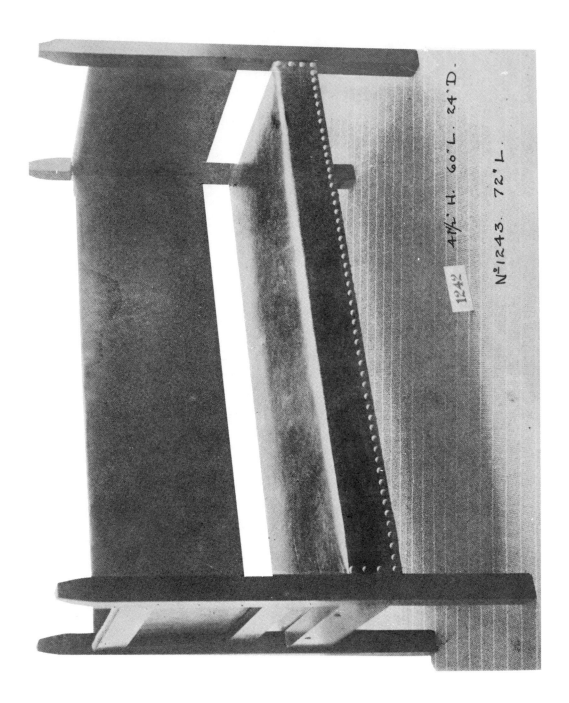

No 1243.   72" L.

4½" H.   60" L.   24" D.

1242

1273

Height of back 40"
  "   " seat 16½"
Size "   " 22" W.
          27" D.

109

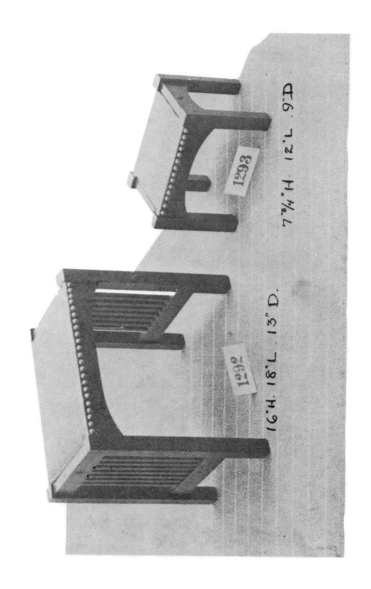

1292
16"H. 18"L. 13"D.

1293
7¾"H. 12"L. 9"D.

110

1301

Height of back 36"
Seat 18"
Size " 18"x18"

1800

Height of back 65"
Seat 18"
Size " 15"x15"

111

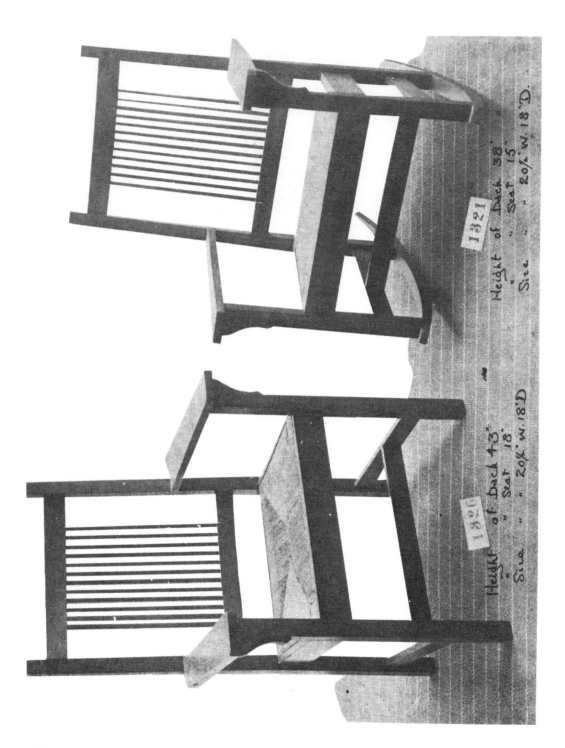

112

Retail Plates, ca. 1909

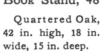

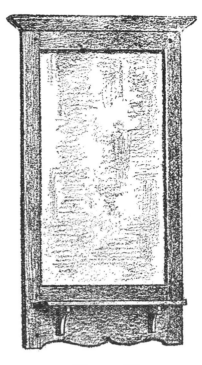

Book Stand, 48

Quartered Oak,
42 in. high, 18 in.
wide, 15 in. deep.

Mirror, 62.

Quartered Oak
or Cuban Mahog-
any. French plate
mirror 14x24 in.

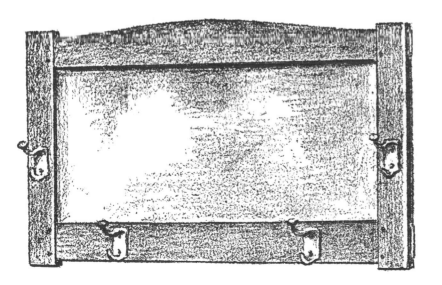

Hall Mirror, 65.

Quartered Oak.
French plate
mirror 18x34 in.
Hand-wrought
copper hooks.

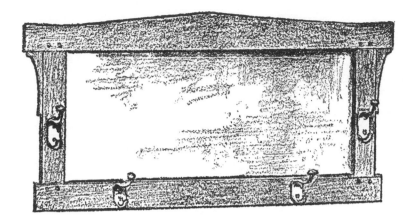

Hall Mirror, 66.
Quartered Oak.
French plate
mirror 16x30 in.
Handwrought cop-
per hooks.

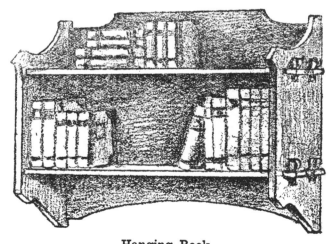

**Hanging Book
Shelf, 80.**
Quartered Oak.
30 in. long, 22 in.
high, 8 in. deep.

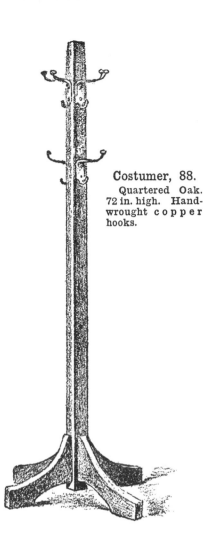

Costumer, 88.
Quartered Oak.
72 in. high. Hand-
wrought copper
hooks.

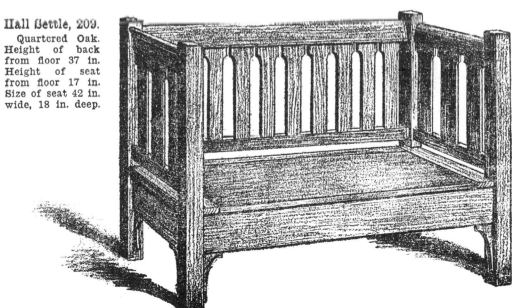

Hall Settle, 209.
Quartered Oak.
Height of back
from floor 37 in.
Height of seat
from floor 17 in.
Size of seat 42 in.
wide, 18 in. deep.

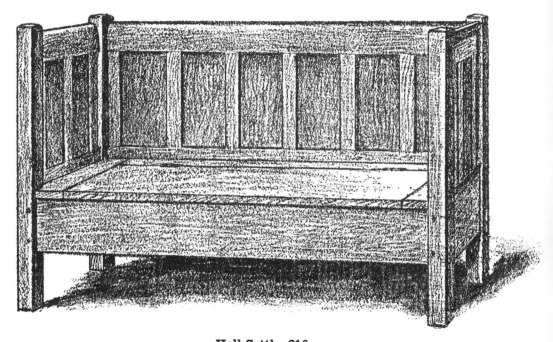

Hall Settle, 210.

Quartered Oak.
Height of back
from floor 37 in.
Height of seat
from floor 17 in.
Size of seat 54
in. wide, 20 in.
deep.

Swing, 217.

54 in. long, 22
in. deep, 30 in.
high. Cushions in
Handcraft canvas
or leather. Hand-
wrought trim-
mings.

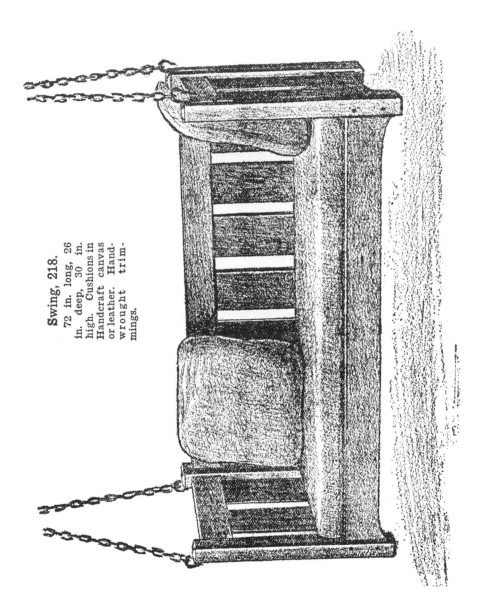

Swing, 218.
72 in. long, 26 in. deep, 30 in. high. Cushions in Handcraft canvas or leather. Hand-wrought trimmings.

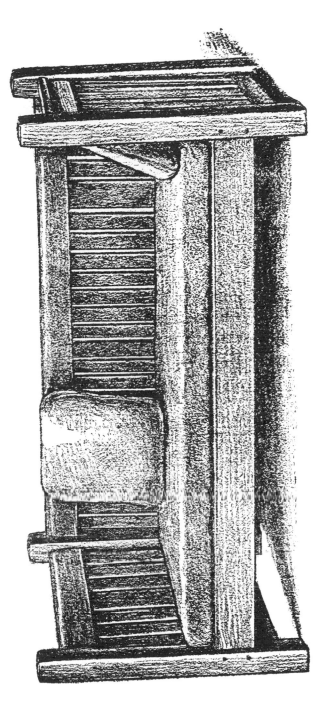

Settle, 223. Quartered Oak or Cuban Mahogany. 84 in. long, 32 in. deep, 39 in. high. Cushions in Handcraft canvas or leather.

Settle, 236.

Quartered Oak
or Cuban Mahogany. Height of
back from floor
41 in. Height of
seat from floor
17 in. Size of
seat 48 in. wide,
22 in. deep. Upholstered in Handcraft sole leather.

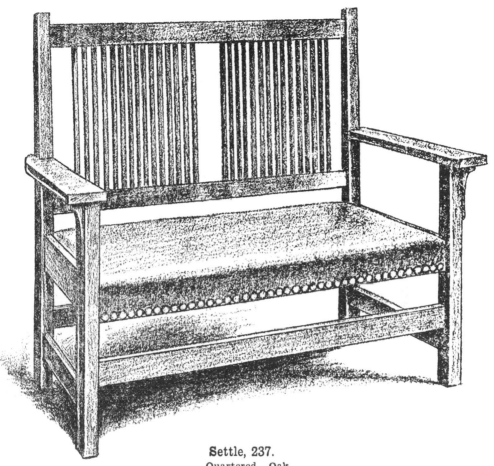

Settle, 237.

Quartered Oak or Cuban Mahogany. Height of back from floor 41 in. Height of seat from floor 17 in. Size of seat 18 in. wide, 22 in. deep. Upholstered in Handcraft sole leather.

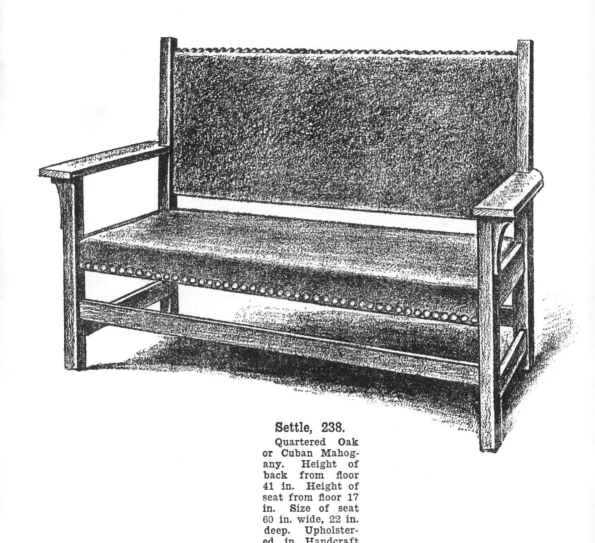

Settle, 238.
Quartered Oak
or Cuban Mahog-
any. Height of
back from floor
41 in. Height of
seat from floor 17
in. Size of seat
60 in. wide, 22 in.
deep. Upholster-
ed in Handcraft
sole leather.

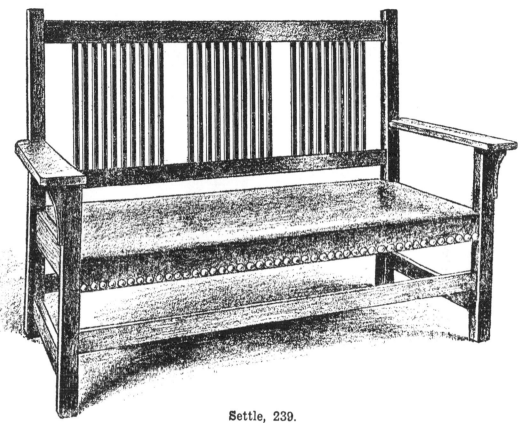

Settle, 239.
Quartered Oak
or Cuban Mahog-
any. 60 in. long,
41 in. high, 22 in.
deep. Upholster-
ed in Handcraft
sole leather.

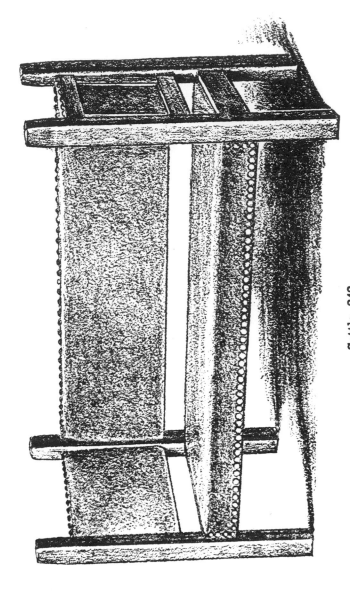

Settle, 242.
Quartered Oak
or Cuban Mahog-
any. 60 in. long,
24 in. deep, 39 in.
high. Upholster-
ed in Handcraft
sole leather.

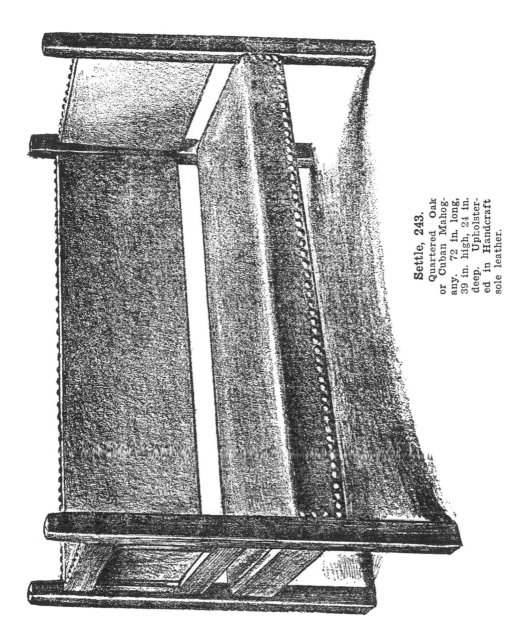

Settle, 243.
Quartered Oak or Cuban Mahogany. 72 in. long, 39 in. high, 24 in. deep. Upholstered in Handcraft sole leather.

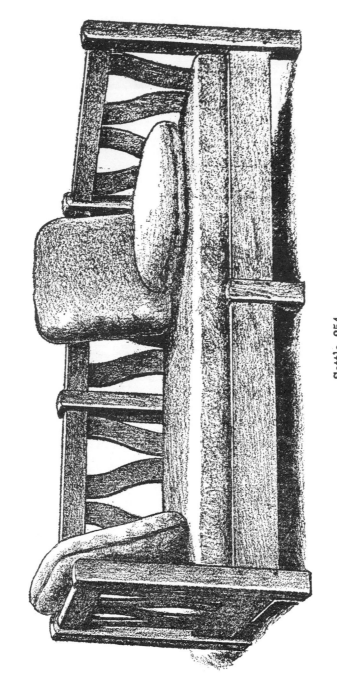

Settle, 254.
Quartered Oak. 78 in. long, 31 in. high, 33 in. deep. Cushions in Handcraft canvas or leather.

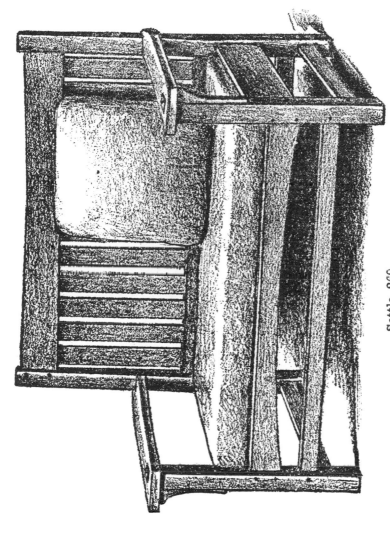

Settle, 260.
Quartered Oak or Cuban Mahogany. 48 in. long, 38 in. high, 23 in. deep. Cushions in Handcraft canvas or leather.

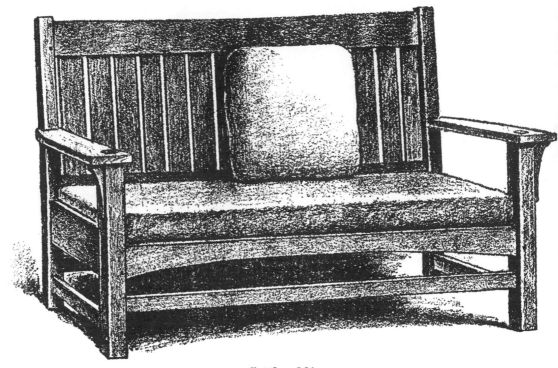

Settle, 261.
Quartered Oak or Cuban Mahogany. 60 in. long, 38 in. high, 24 in. deep. Cushions in Handcraft canvas or leather.

Settle, 284.
Quartered Oak.
48 in. long, 39 in.
high, 22 in. deep.
Upholstered in
Handcraft sole
leather.

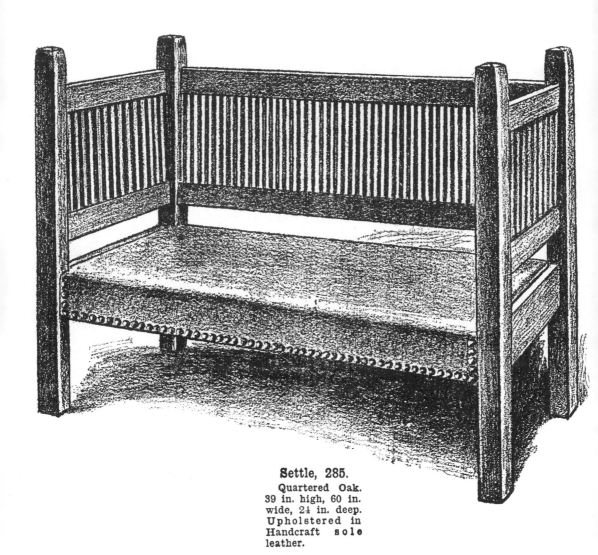

Settle, 285.
Quartered Oak.
39 in. high, 60 in.
wide, 24 in. deep.
Upholstered in
Handcraft sole
leather.

Dining Chair, 300.

Quartered Oak. Height of back from floor 35 in. Height of seat from floor 18 in. Size of seat 18 in. wide, 17 in. deep. Upholstered in Handcraft sole leather.

Arm Chair 301 to match.

Dining Chair, 302.

Quartered Oak or Cuban Mahogany. Height of back from floor 40 in. Height of seat from floor 18 in. Size of seat 17 in. wide, 16 in. deep. Upholstered in Handcraft sole leather.

Arm chair 310 to match.

Dining Chair, 304.

Quartered Oak or Cuban Mahogany. Height of back from floor 40 in., height of seat from floor, 18 in., size of seat 17 in. wide, 16 in. deep. Upholstered in Handcraft sole leather. Arm chair, 312, to match.

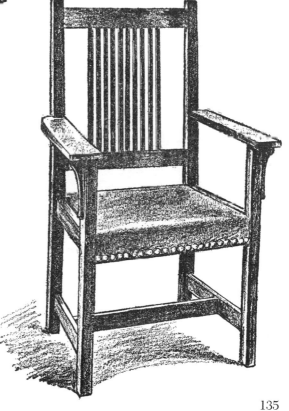

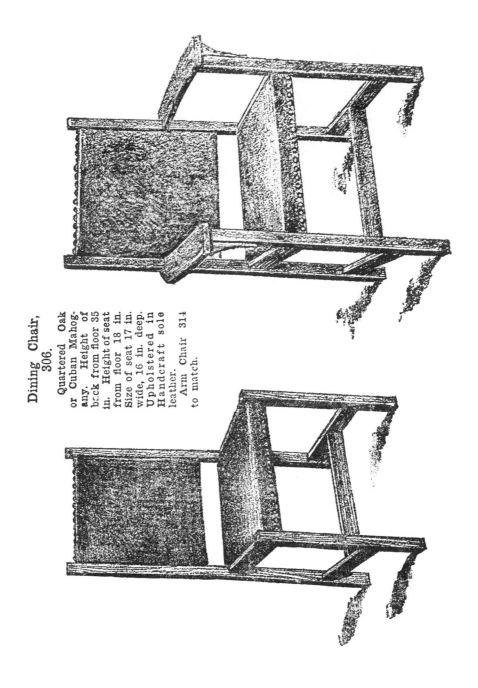

Dining Chair, 306.

Quartered Oak or Cuban Mahogany. Height of back from floor 35 in. Height of seat from floor 18 in. Size of seat 17 in. wide, 16 in. deep. Upholstered in Handcraft sole leather.

Arm Chair 314 to match.

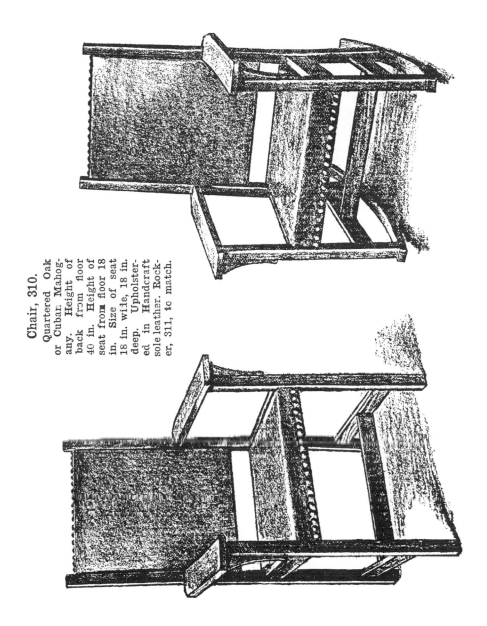

Chair, 310.

Quartered Oak or Cuban Mahogany. Height of back from floor 40 in. Height of seat from floor 18 in. Size of seat 18 in. wide, 18 in. deep. Upholstered in Handcraft sole leather. Rocker, 311, to match.

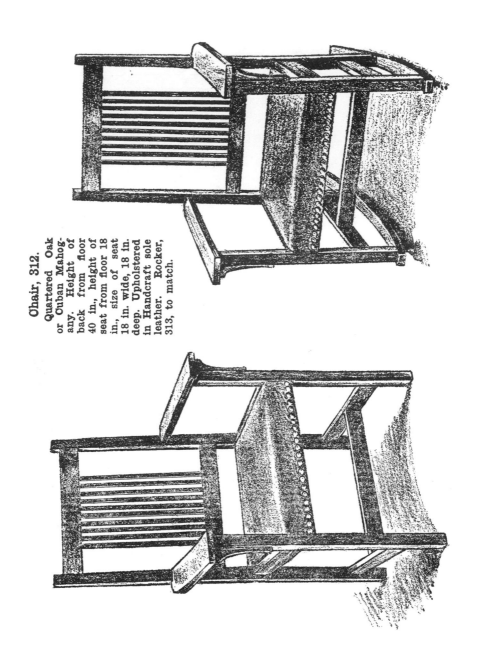

Chair, 312.
Quartered Oak or Cuban Mahogany. Height of back from floor 40 in., height of seat from floor 18 in., size of seat 18 in. wide, 18 in. deep. Upholstered in Handcraft sole leather. Rocker, 313, to match.

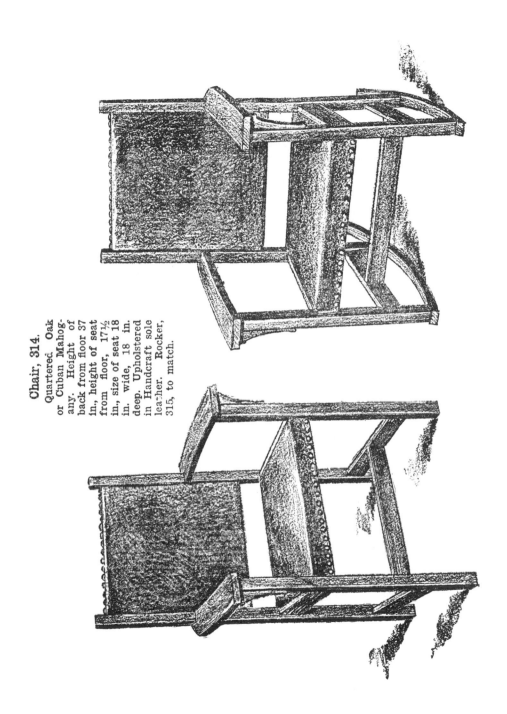

Chair, 314.
Quartered Oak or Cuban Mahogany. Height of back from floor 37 in., height of seat from floor, 17½ in., size of seat 18 in. wide, 18 in. deep. Upholstered in Handcraft sole leather. Rocker, 315, to match.

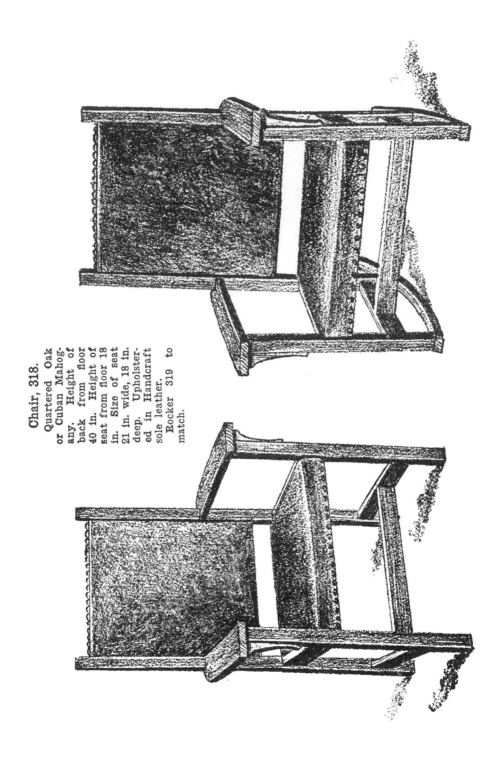

Chair, 318.
Quartered Oak or Cuban Mahogany. Height of back from floor 40 in. Height of seat from floor 18 in. Size of seat 21 in. wide, 18 in. deep. Upholstered in Handcraft sole leather. Rocker 319 to match.

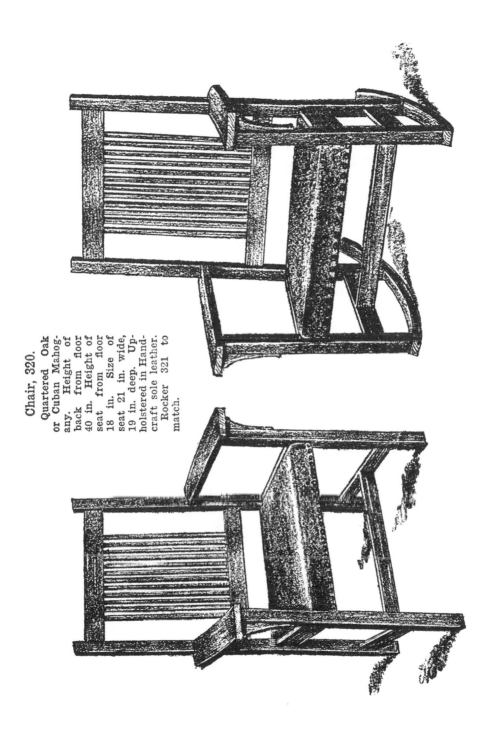

Chair, 320.
Quartered Oak or Cuban Mahogany. Height of back from floor 40 in. Height of seat from floor 18 in. Size of seat 21 in. wide, 19 in. deep. Upholstered in Handcraft sole leather. Rocker 321 to match.

Chair, 326.

Quartered Oak. Height of back from floor 38 in. Height of seat from floor 18 in. Size of seat 21 in. wide, 19 in. deep. Upholstered in Handcraft sole leather. Rocker 327 to match.

328

Desk Chair, 328.

Quartered Oak or Cuban Mahogany. Height of back from floor 36 in. Height of seat from floor 18 in. Size of seat 16 in. wide, 14 in. deep. Upholstered in Handcraft sole leather.

Desk Chair, 330.

Same dimensions as 328.

330

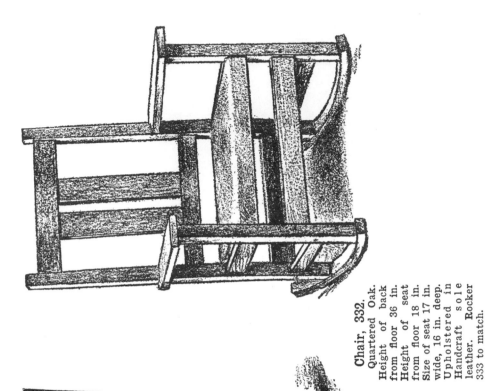

Chair, 332.
Quartered Oak.
Height of back
from floor 36 in.
Height of seat
from floor 18 in.
Size of seat 17 in.
wide, 16 in. deep.
Upholstered in
Handcraft sole
leather. Rocker
333 to match.

Rocker, 333.
Quartered Oak. Height of back from floor 36 in. Height of seat from floor 16 in. Size of seat 17 in. wide, 16 in. deep. Upholstered in Handcraft sole leather. Arm Rocker 335 to match.

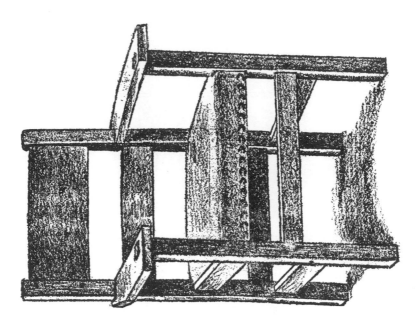

Dining Chair, 341.

Quartered Oak. Height of back from floor 36 in. Height of seat from floor 18 in. Size of seat 19 in. wide, 17 in. deep. Upholstered in Handcraft sole leather.

Arm Chair 342 to match.

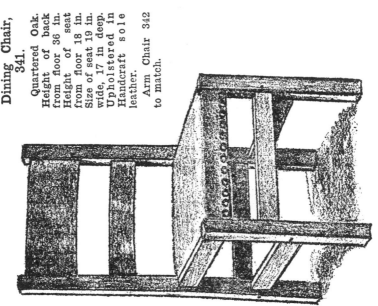

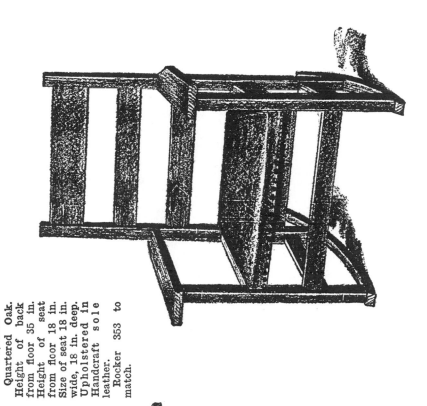

Chair, 352.
Quartered Oak.
Height of back from floor 35 in.
Height of seat from floor 18 in.
Size of seat 18 in. wide, 18 in. deep.
Upholstered in Handcraft sole leather.
Rocker 353 to match.

147

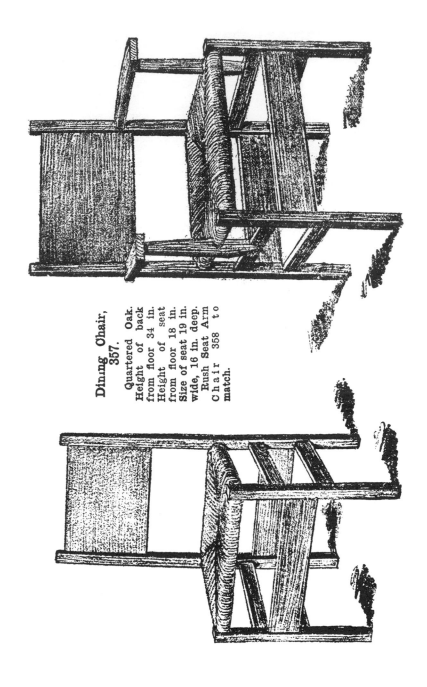

Dining Chair, 357.

Quartered Oak. Height of back from floor 34 in. Height of seat from floor 18 in. Size of seat 19 in. wide, 16 in. deep. Rush Seat Arm Chair 358 to match.

148

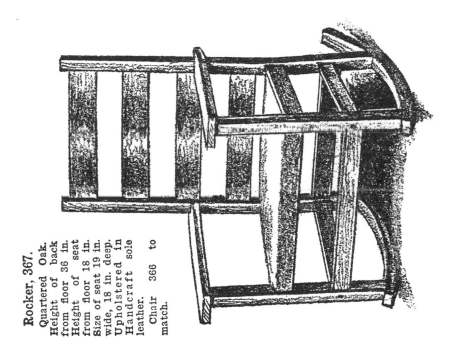

Rocker, 367.
Quartered Oak.
Height of back
from floor 36 in.
Height of seat
from floor 18 in.
Size of seat 19 in.
wide, 18 in. deep.
Upholstered in
Handcraft sole
leather. Chair 366 to
match.

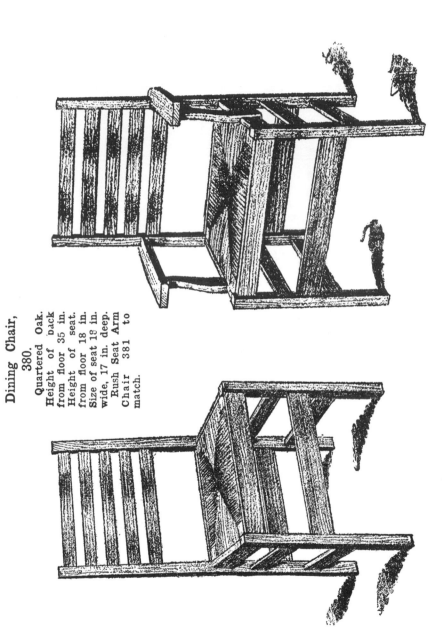

Dining Chair, 380.

Quartered Oak. Height of back from floor 35 in. Height of seat. from floor 18 in. Size of seat 18 in. wide, 17 in. deep. Rush Seat Arm Chair 381 to match.

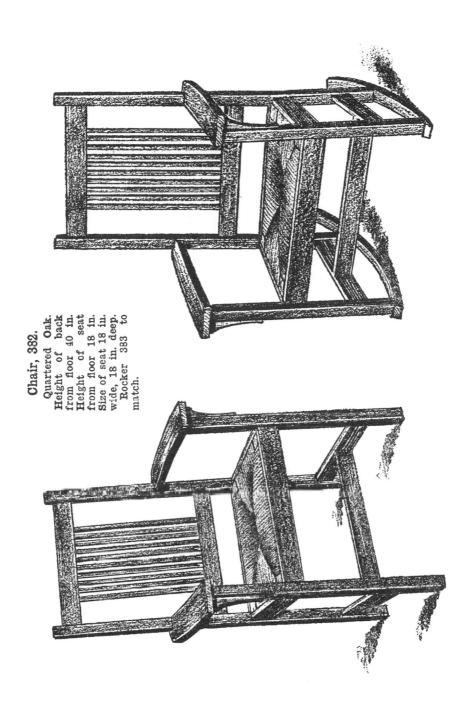

Chair, 382.
Quartered Oak.
Height of back
from floor 40 in.
Height of seat
from floor 18 in.
Size of seat 18 in.
wide, 18 in. deep.
Rocker 383 to
match.

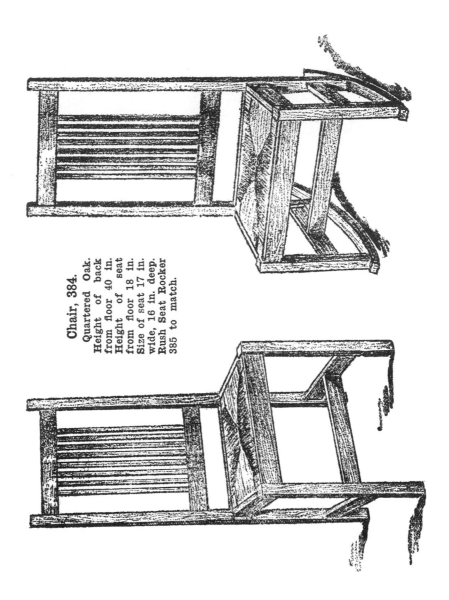

Chair, 384.
Quartered Oak.
Height of back
from floor 40 in.
Height of seat
from floor 18 in.
Size of seat 17 in.
wide, 16 in. deep.
Rush Seat Rocker
385 to match.

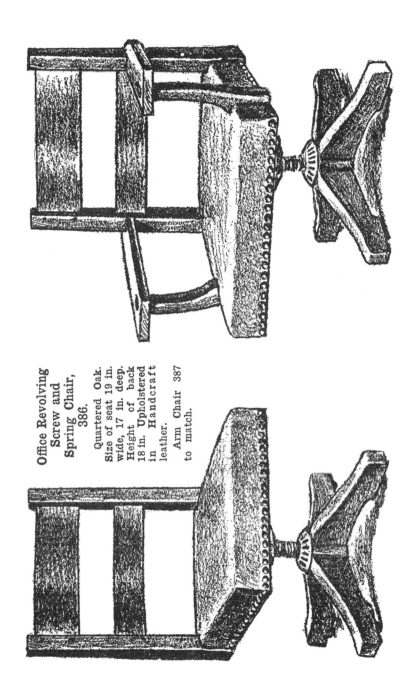

Office Revolving Screw and Spring Chair, 386.

Quartered Oak. Size of seat 19 in. wide, 17 in. deep. Height of back 18 in. Upholstered in Handcraft leather.

Arm Chair 387 to match.

390

Seat or Foot Rest, 390.

Quartered Oak. 18 in. high, 30 in. long, 17 in. deep. Upholstered in Handcraft sole leather.

Foot Rest, 391.

Quartered Oak. 18 in. high, 18 in. long, 14 in. deep. Upholstered in Handcraft sole leather.

391

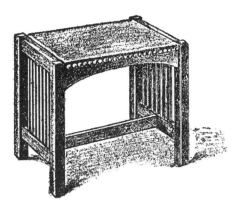

Foot Rest, 392.

Quartered Oak or Cuban Mahogany. 16 in. high, 13 in. wide, 18 in. long. Upholstered in Handcraft sole leather.

Foot Rest, 394.

Quartered Oak. 16 in. high, 15 in. wide, 19 in. long. Upholstered in Handcraft canvas or leather.

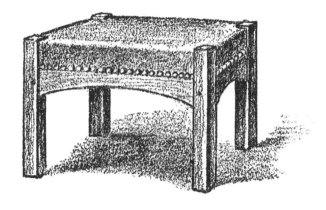

Foot Rest, 395.

Quartered Oak. 9 in. high, 19 in. wide, 13 in. deep. Upholstered in Handcraft canvas or leather.

155

Reading Chair, 411.

Quartered Oak. Height of back from floor 41 in. Height of seat from floor 16 in. Size of seat 24 in. wide, 26 in. deep. Cushions in Handcraft canvas or leather.

Chair, 420.

Quartered Oak
or Cuban Mahog-
any. Height of
back from floor
40 in., height of
seat from floor 17
in., size of seat
22 in. wide, 24 in.
deep. Cushions in
Handcraft canvas
or leather.

Chair, 430.

Quartered Oak. Height of back from floor 30 in., height of seat from floor 14 in., size of seat 24 in. wide, 28 in. deep. Cushions in Handcraft canvas or leather.

Rocker, 431.

Quartered Oak. Height of back from floor 30 in., height of seat from floor 14 in., size of seat 24 in. wide, 28 in. deep. Cushions in Handcraft canvas or leather.

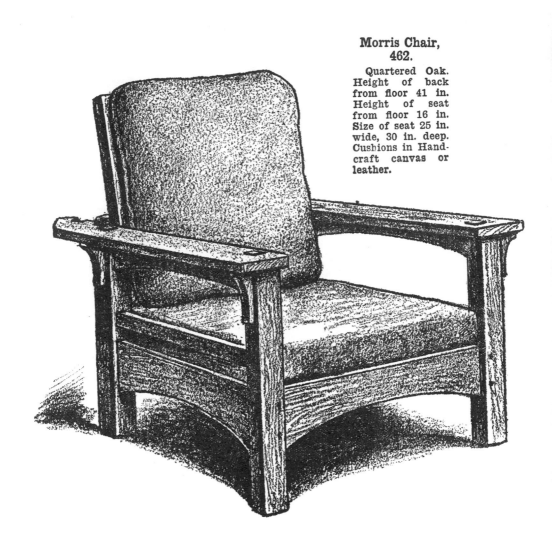

Morris Chair, 462.

Quartered Oak. Height of back from floor 41 in. Height of seat from floor 16 in. Size of seat 25 in. wide, 30 in. deep. Cushions in Handcraft canvas or leather.

**Morris Chair,
468.**

Quartered Oak.
Height of back
from floor 41 in.
Height of seat
from floor 16 in.
Size of seat 23 in.
wide, 26 in deep.
Cushions in Hand-
craft canvas or
leather.

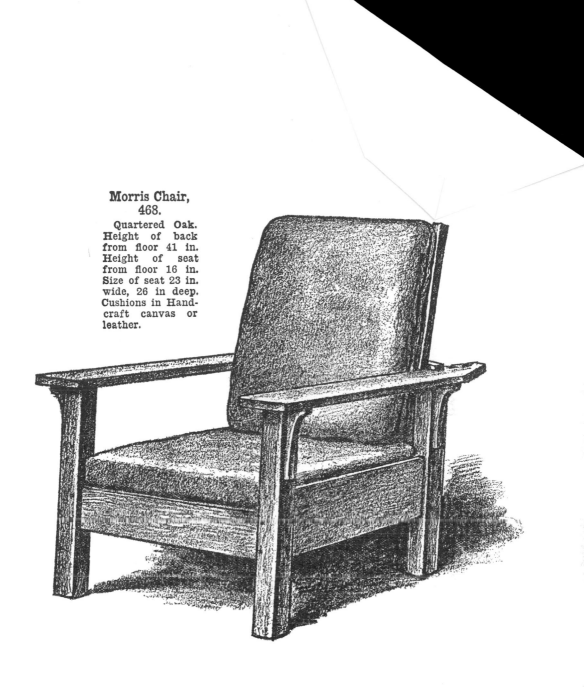

Morris Chair, 470.

Quartered Oak. Height of back from floor 41 in. Height of seat from floor 16 in. Size of seat 24 in. wide, 26 in. deep. Cushions in Handcraft canvas or leather.

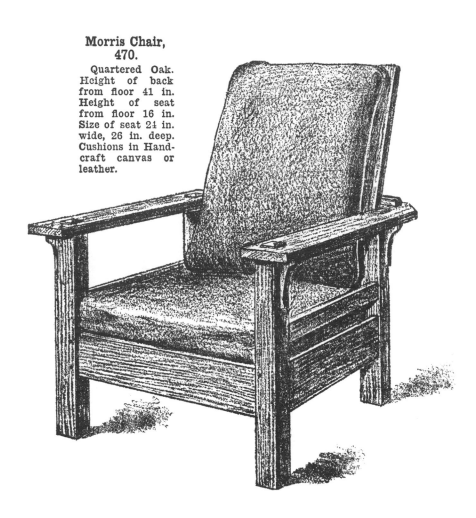

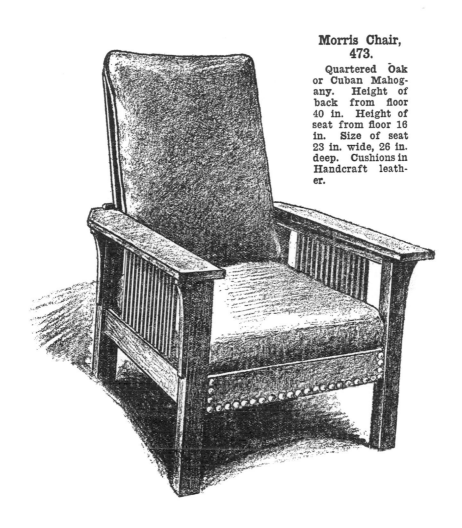

Morris Chair, 473.

Quartered Oak or Cuban Mahogany. Height of back from floor 40 in. Height of seat from floor 16 in. Size of seat 23 in. wide, 26 in. deep. Cushions in Handcraft leather.

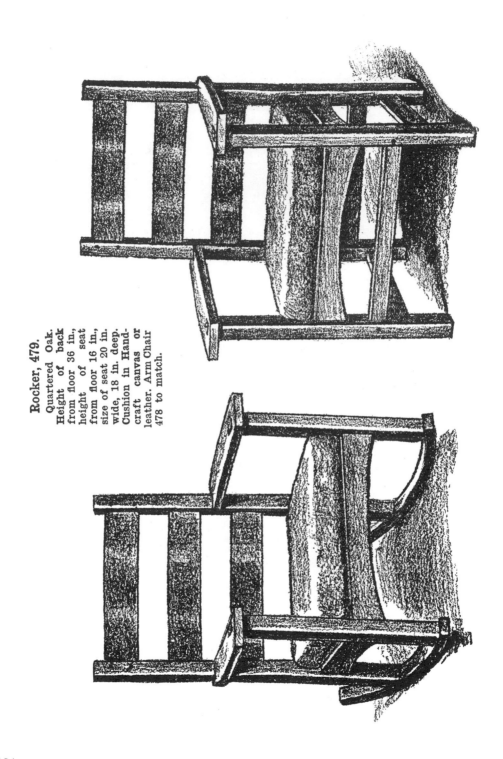

Rocker, 479.
Quartered Oak. Height of back from floor 36 in., height of seat from floor 16 in., size of seat 20 in. wide, 18 in. deep. Cushion in Handcraft canvas or leather. Arm Chair 478 to match.

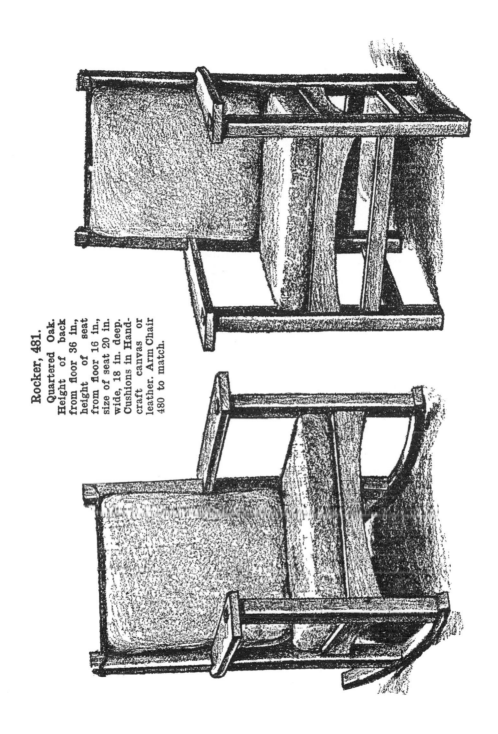

Rocker, 481.
Quartered Oak. Height of back from floor 36 in., height of seat from floor 16 in., size of seat 20 in. wide, 18 in. deep. Cushions in Handcraft canvas or leather. Arm Chair 480 to match.

165

Rocker, 485.

Quartered Oak.
Height of back
from floor 48 in.
Height of seat
from floor 17 in.
Size of seat 22 in.
wide, 24 in. deep.

**Tea Table
(square), 507.**
Quartered Oak.
Top 17x26 in., 24
in. high.

**Tea Table
(round), 508.**
Quartered Oak.
Top 24x24 in., 24
in. high.

Smokers' Table, 515.

Quartered Oak. Top 20x20 in., 24 in. high.

Table, 521.

Quartered Oak or Cuban Mahogany. Top 28x42 in., 29 in. high. Hand-wrought copper pulls. Wood or leather top.

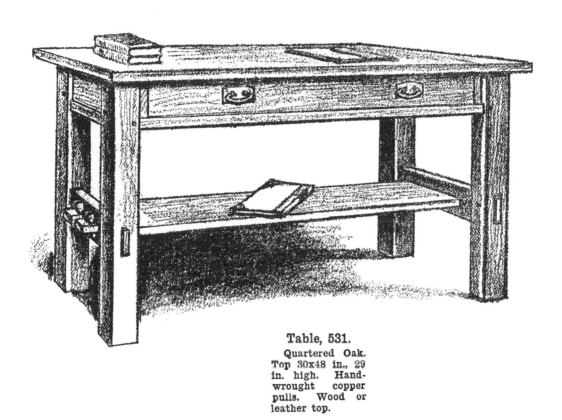

Table, 531.
Quartered Oak.
Top 30x48 in., 29
in. high. Hand-
wrought copper
pulls. Wood or
leather top.

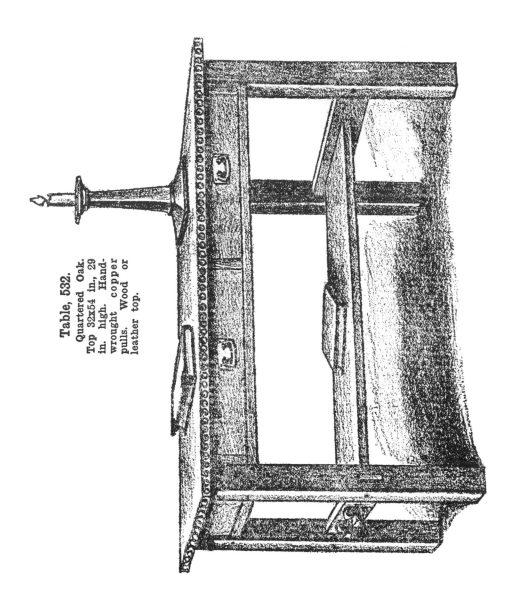

Table, 532.
Quartered Oak.
Top 32x54 in., 29
in. high. Hand-
wrought copper
pulls. Wood or
leather top.

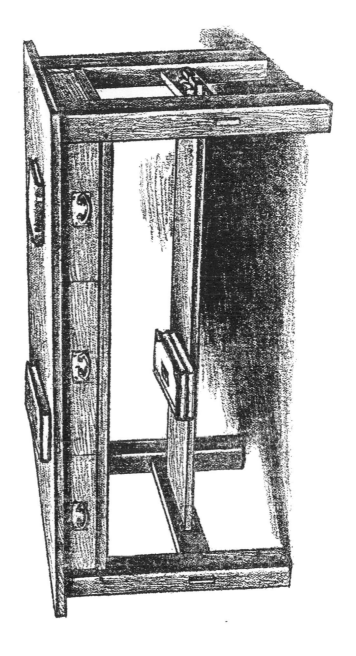

Table, 533.
Quartered Oak. Top 32x60 in, 29 in. high. Hand-wrought copper pulls. Wood or leather top.

Table, 536.
Quartered Oak.
Top 24x24 in., 29
in. high.

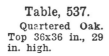
Table, 537.
Quartered Oak.
Top 36x36 in., 29
in. high.

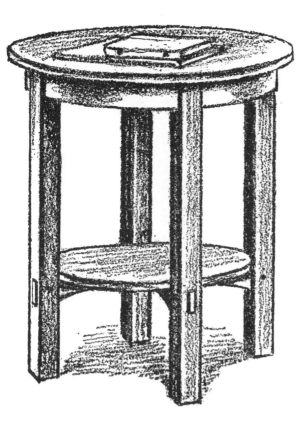

Table, 540.
Quartered Oak.
Top 24x24 in., 29
in. high. Wood
or leather top.

Table, 542.
Quartered Oak.
Top 36x36 in., 29
in high. Wood or
leather top.

Table, 544.
Quartered Oak.
Top 48x48 in., 29
in high. Wood or
leather top.

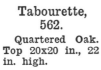

**Tabourette,
562.**
Quartered Oak.
Top 20x20 in., 22
in. high.

Table, 564.
Quartered Oak.
Top 54x54 in., 30
in. high. Wood or
leather top.

Table, 582.
Quartered Oak or Cuban Mahogany. Top 30x48 in., 29 in. high. Hand-wrought copper pulls. Wood or leather top.

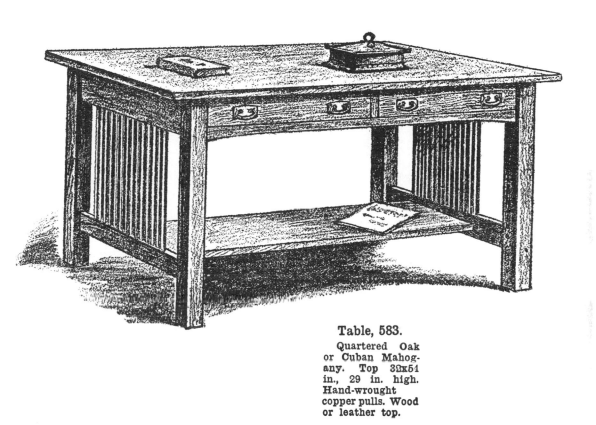

Table, 583.

Quartered Oak
or Cuban Mahog-
any. Top 32x54
in., 29 in. high.
Hand-wrought
copper pulls. Wood
or leather top.

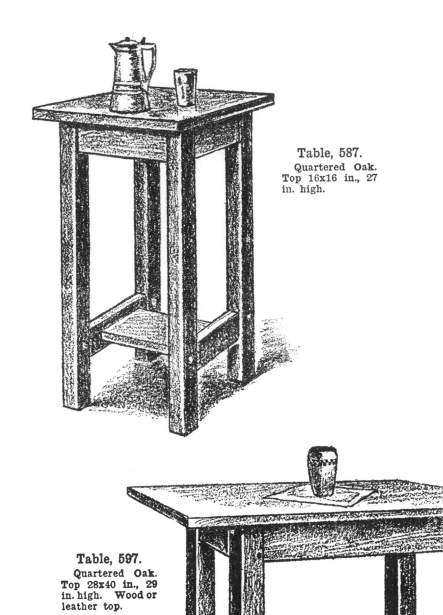

Table, 587.
Quartered Oak.
Top 16x16 in., 27
in. high.

Table, 597.
Quartered Oak.
Top 28x40 in., 29
in. high. Wood or
leather top.

Writing Desk, 602.

Quartered Oak.
35 in. high, 40 in.
wide, 22 in. deep.
Hand-wrought cop-
per pulls.

**Writing Desk,
604.**

Quartered Oak.
36 in. high, 40 in.
wide, 22 in. deep.
Hand-wrought cop-
per pulls.

**Open Book
Case, 642.**

Quartered Oak.
55 in. high, 30 in.
wide, 12 in. deep.

**Open Book
Case, 644.**

Quartered Oak.
55 in. high, 36 in.
wide, 12 in. deep.

**Open Book
Case, 646.**

Quartered Oak.
55 in. high, 49 in.
wide, 12 in. deep.

**Open Book
Case, 648.**

Quartered Oak.
55 in. high, 70 in.
wide, 12 in. deep.

**Writing Desk,
664.**

Quartered Oak.
47 in. high, 36 in.
wide, 19 in. deep.
Hand-wrought
copper pulls.

Writing Desk,
664, Open.
Same as 664.

Sideboard, 704.
Quartered Oak. 54 in. high, 48 in. wide, 20 in. deep. Same Sideboard, 703, with plate rail.

China Cabinet,
705.

Quartered Oak.
68 in. high, 42 in.
wide, 16 in. deep.